Presenting

C#

Christoph Wille

SAMS *A Division of Macmillan USA*
201 West 103rd St., Indianapolis, Indiana, 46290 USA

Presenting C#

Copyright © 2000 by Sams Publishing

International Standard Book Number: 0-672-32037-1

Library of Congress Catalog Card Number: 00-105188

Printed in the United States of America

First Printing: July 2000

02   01   00   4   3   2   1

Trademarks

Warning and Disclaimer

ASSOCIATE PUBLISHER
Bradley L. Jones

EXECUTIVE EDITOR
Chris Webb

DEVELOPMENT EDITOR
Kevin Howard

MANAGING EDITOR
Charlotte Clapp

PROJECT EDITOR
Carol L. Bowers

COPY EDITOR
Michael Henry

INDEXER
Chris Barrick

PROOFREADER
Carol L. Bowers
Charlotte Clapp

COVER DESIGNER
Alan Clements

BOOK DESIGNER
Gary Adair

Overview

Table of Contents

Acknowledgements

What would you expect when you receive an email from an executive editor, mentioning that he wants to talk with you about an exciting book project? I didn't quite expect this book when Chris Webb called me. Chris's offer was way too exciting to turn down—writing a book about a new programming language.

Thanks to both Chris Webb and Brad Jones (the associate publisher) for putting their trust in me and my tight writing schedule. Both of them—as well as the development editor, Kevin Howard—had to put up with my changes to the table of contents as the book progressed. You just can't kill old habits.

Special thanks to Christian Koller for reviewing my chapters and telling me when I once again left out details that non-C++ programmers would need for better understanding. Although I don't know everyone who was involved in this book project at Sams Publishing, I thank them all for bringing it to the shelves—especially within this tight schedule!

Finally, and of course most importantly, I want to thank my family for their continual support throughout all my book projects.

About the Author

Christoph Wille, MCSE, MCSD, CNA, and MCP-IT, works as a network consultant and programmer, and specializes in Windows DNA. He is recognized by Microsoft as a Most Valuable Professional (MVP) for Active Server Pages, and was one of only a handful of developers working with Microsoft on early versions of the C# language.

Christoph has authored or contributed to several books, including *Sams Teach Yourself ADO 2.5 in 21 Days*, *Sams Teach Yourself Active Server Pages in 24 Hours*, *MCSE Training Guide: SQL Server 7 Administration*, and *Sams Teach Yourself MCSE TCP/IP in 14 Days*.

Tell Us What You Think!

As the reader of this book, *you* are our most important critic and commentator. We value your opinion and want to know what we're doing right, what we could do better, what areas you'd like to see us publish in, and any other words of wisdom you're willing to pass our way.

As an Associate Publisher for Sams, I welcome your comments. You can fax, email, or write me directly to let me know what you did or didn't like about this book—as well as what we can do to make our books stronger.

Please note that I cannot help you with technical problems related to the topic of this book, and that due to the high volume of mail I receive, I might not be able to reply to every message.

When you write, please be sure to include this book's title and author as well as your name and phone or fax number. I will carefully review your comments and share them with the author and editors who worked on the book.

Fax: 317-581-4770

Email: adv_prog@mcp.com

Mail: Bradley L. Jones
          Associate Publisher
          Sams Publishing
          201 West 103rd Street
          Indianapolis, IN 46290 USA

INTRODUCTION

Welcome to *Presenting C#*. This book is your ticket to quickly getting up to speed with the enterprise programming language that ships with the Next Generation Windows Services (NGWS) Runtime: C# (pronounced C sharp).

The Next Generation Windows Services Runtime is a runtime environment that not only manages the execution of code, but also provides services that make programming easier. Compilers produce managed code to target this managed execution environment. You get cross-language integration, cross-language exception handling, enhanced security, versioning and deployment support, and debugging and profiling services for free.

The premier language for the NGWS Runtime is C#. Much of the supporting NGWS framework is written in C#; therefore, its compiler can be considered the most tested and optimized compiler of those shipping with the NGWS Runtime. The C# language borrows power from C++, but with modernization and the addition of type safety—making C# the number one choice for enterprise solutions.

Who Should Read This Book?

If you are new to programming, this book is not for you. This book is intended to get programmers off and running with C#, based on knowledge that they already have. *Presenting C#* is targeted at programmers who already have programming experience in, for example, C or C++, Visual Basic, Java, or another language.

The transition to C# is easiest when you have a background in C++; however, if you are fluent in a different language, this book will bring you up to date, too. The book is more fun if you have a little knowledge of COM programming, but COM programming is in no way mandatory.

How This Book Is Organized

The book is organized into twelve chapters. Here is a quick rundown on what is presented in each chapter:

- Chapter 1, "Introduction to C#"—You are taken on a tour of C#, and this chapter answers questions about why you should consider learning C#.

- Chapter 2, "The Underpinnings—The NGWS Runtime"—You are introduced to how the NGWS Runtime provides the infrastructure for your C# code to run.

- Chapter 3, "Your First C# Application"—You create your very first C# application and (how could it be otherwise?) it is a "Hello World" application.

- Chapter 4, "C# Types"—You discover the various types that you can use in your C# applications. You explore the differences between value types and reference types, and how boxing and unboxing works.

- Chapter 5, "Classes"—You tap the real power of C#, which is object-oriented programming with classes. You learn a great deal about constructors, destructors, methods, properties, indexers, and events.

- Chapter 6, "Control Statements"—You take over the control of flow in your application. You explore the various selection and iteration statements provided by C#.

- Chapter 7, "Exception Handling"—You acquire the skills to write applications that are good citizens in the world of the NGWS Runtime, by implementing proper exception handling.

- Chapter 8, "Writing Components in C#"—You build a component in C# that can be used by clients across languages because you leverage the NGWS Runtime.

- Chapter 9, "Configuration and Deployment"—You learn how conditional compilation works in C#, as well as how to automatically generate documentation from your C# source code. Additionally, this chapter introduces the versioning technology of NGWS.

- Chapter 10, "Interoperating with Unmanaged Code"—You discover how you can use unmanaged code from inside C#, and how unmanaged code can interoperate with your C# components.

- Chapter 11, "Debugging C# Code"—You acquire the skills to use the debugging tools provided in the SDK to pinpoint and fix bugs in your C# applications.

- Chapter 12, "Security"—You explore the security concepts of the NGWS Runtime. You learn about code-access security and role-based security.

What You Will Need to Use This Book

From the book's point of view, all you need is the Next Generation
Windows Services (NGWS) Software Development Kit (SDK). Although
all you need at a minimum are the NGWS Runtime and the C# compiler,
having a machine loaded with the documentation and all the SDK's tools
(including its debugger) is definitely a good idea when exploring the
capabilities of this exciting new technology.

This book does not require you to have any of the Visual Studio 7 tools
installed on your machine. My only recommendation is that you should
have a decent programmer's editor that supports line numbering for
editing C# source files.

CHAPTER 1

Introduction to C#

- Why Another Programming Language?

Welcome to the world of C#! This chapter takes you on a tour of C# and answers questions such as why you should use C#, what the main differences are between C++ and C#, and why C# will make development easier and more fun for you.

Why Another Programming Language?

A good question that has to be answered is why you should learn another programming language when you are already doing enterprise development in C++ or Visual Basic. The marketing-type answer is that "C# is intended to be the premier language for writing NGWS (Next Generation Windows Services) applications in the enterprise computing space." This chapter is about backing up that claim with arguments, and showcasing a slew of C#'s features. This chapter is about whetting your appetite.

The programming language C# derives from C and C++; however, it is modern, simple, entirely object-oriented, and type-safe. If you are a C/C++ programmer, your learning curve will be flat. Many C# statements are directly borrowed from your favorite language, including expressions and operators. If you don't look too closely at first, a C# program looks like a C++ program.

An important point about C# is that it is a modern programming language. It simplifies and modernizes C++ in the areas of classes, namespaces, method overloading, and exception handling. Much of the complexity of C++ was removed from C# to make it easier to use and less error prone.

Contributing to the ease of use is the elimination of certain features of C++: no more macros, no templates, and no multiple inheritance. The aforementioned features create more problems than they provide benefit—especially for enterprise developers.

New features for added convenience are strict type safety, versioning, garbage collection, and many more. All these features are targeted at developing component-oriented software. Although you don't have the sheer power of C++, you become more productive faster.

Before I get ahead of myself and present too many features, I want to stop and present the various elements of C# based on key points in the following sections:

- Simple

- Modern

- Object-oriented
- Type-safe
- Versionable
- Compatible
- Flexible

Simple

One thing you definitely wouldn't attribute to C++ is that learning it is simple. This is not so with C#. The foremost goal for this programming language was simplicity. Many features—or the lack thereof—contribute to the overall simplicity of C#.

Pointers are a prominent feature that is missing in C#. By default, you are working with managed code, where unsafe operations, such as direct memory manipulation, are not allowed. I don't think any C++ programmer can claim never to have accessed memory that didn't belong to him via a pointer.

Closely related to the pointer "drama" is operator "madness." In C++, you have : :, ., and -> operators that are used for namespaces, members, and references. For a beginner, operators make for yet another hard day of learning. C# does away with the different operators in favor of a single one: the . (the "dot"). All that a programmer now has to understand is the notion of nested names.

You no longer have to remember cryptic types that originate from different processor architectures—including varying ranges of integer types. C# does away with them by providing a unified type system. This type system enables you to view every type as an object, be it a primitive type or a full-blown class. In contrast to other programming languages, treating a simple type as an object does not come with a performance penalty because of a mechanism called boxing and unboxing. Boxing and unboxing is explained later in detail, but basically, this technique provides object access to simple types only when requested.

At first, seasoned programmers might not like it, but integer and Boolean data types are now finally two entirely different types. That means a mistaken assignment in an `if` statement is now flagged as an error by the compiler because it takes a Boolean result only. No more comparison-versus-assignment errors!

C# also gets rid of redundancies that crept into C++ over the years. Such redundancies include, for example, `const` versus `#define`, different character types, and so on. Commonly used forms are available in C#, whereas the redundant forms were eliminated from the language.

Modern

The effort you put into learning C# is a great investment because C# was designed to be the premier language for writing NGWS applications. You will find many features that you had to implement yourself in C++, or that were simply unavailable, are part of the base C# language implementation.

The financial types are a welcome addition for an enterprise-level programming language. You get a new `decimal` data type that is targeted at monetary calculations. If you are not fond of the provided simple types, you can easily create new ones specifically crafted for your application.

I have already mentioned that pointers are no longer part of your programming weaponry. You won't be too surprised then that the entire memory management is no longer your duty—the runtime of NGWS provides a garbage collector that is responsible for memory management in your C# programs. Because memory and your application are managed, it is imperative that type safety be enforced to guarantee application stability.

It is not exactly news to C++ programmers, but exception handling is a main feature of C#. The difference from C++, however, is that exception handling is cross-language (another feature of the runtime). Prior to C#, you had to deal with quirky `HRESULT`s—this is now over because of robust error handling that is based on exceptions.

Security is a top requirement for a modern application. C# won't leave you alone on this either: It provides metadata syntax for declaring capabilities and permissions for the underlying NGWS security model. Metadata is a key concept of the NGWS runtime, and the next chapter deals with its implications in more depth.

Object-Oriented

You wouldn't expect a new language to not support object-oriented features, would you? C#, of course, supports all the key object-oriented concepts such as encapsulation, inheritance, and polymorphism. The entire C# class model is built on top of the NGWS runtime's Virtual Object System (VOS), which is described in the next chapter. The object model is part of the infrastructure, and is no longer part of the programming language.

One thing you will notice right from the start is that there are no more global functions, variables, or constants. Everything must be encapsulated inside a class, either as an instance member (accessible via an instance of a class—an object) or a static member (via the type). This makes your C# code more readable and also helps to reduce potential naming conflicts.

The methods you can define on classes are, by default, nonvirtual (they cannot be overridden by deriving classes). The main point of this is that another source of errors disappears—the accidental overriding of methods. For a method to be able to be overridden, it must have the explicit `virtual` modifier. This behavior not only reduces the size of the virtual function table, but also guarantees correct versioning behavior.

When you are used to programming classes in C++, you know that you can set different access levels for class members by using access modifiers. C# also supports the `private`, `protected`, and `public` access modifiers, and also adds a fourth one: `internal`. Details about these access modifiers are presented in Chapter 5, "Classes."

How many of you have ever created a class that derives from multiple base classes? (ATL programmers, your vote doesn't count!) In most cases, you need to derive from only one class. Multiple base classes usually add more problems than they solve. That is why C# allows only one base class. If you feel the need for multiple inheritance, you can implement interfaces.

A question that might come up is how to emulate function pointers when there are no pointers in C#. The answer to this question is *delegates*, which provide the underpinnings for the NGWS runtime's event model. Again, I have to put off a full explanation until Chapter 5.

Type-Safe

Once again, I have to pick on pointers as an example. When you had a pointer in C++, you were free to cast it to any type, including doing rather idiotic things such as casting an int* (int pointer) to a double* (double pointer). As long as memory backed that operation, it kind of "worked." This is not the kind of type safety you would envision for an enterprise-level programming language.

Because of the outlined problems, C# implements strictest type safety to protect itself and the garbage collector. Therefore, you must abide by a few rules in C# with regard to variables:

- You cannot use uninitialized variables. For member variables of an object, the compiler takes care of zeroing them. For local variables, you are in charge. However, if you use an uninitialized variable, the compiler will tell you so. The advantage is that you get rid of those errors when using an uninitialized variable to compute a result and you don't know how these funny results are produced.

- C# does away with unsafe casts. You cannot cast from an integer to a reference type (object, for example), and when you downcast, C# verifies that this cast is okay. (That is, that the derived object is really derived from the class to which you are downcasting it.)

- Bounds checking is part of C#. It is no longer possible to use that "extra" array element n, when the array actually has n-1 elements. This makes it impossible to overwrite unallocated memory.

- Arithmetic operations could overflow the range of the result data type. C# allows you to check for overflow in such operations on either an application level or a statement level. With overflow checking enabled, an exception is thrown when an overflow happens.

- Reference parameters that are passed in C# are type-safe.

Versionable

Over the past few years, almost every programmer has had to deal at least once with what has become known as "DLL Hell." The problem stems from the fact that multiple applications install different versions of the same DLL to the computer. Sometimes, older applications happily work with the newer version of the DLL; however, most of the time, they break. Versioning is a real pain today.

As you will see in Chapter 8, "Writing Components in C#," the versioning support for applications you write is provided by the NGWS runtime. C# does its best to support this versioning. Although C# itself cannot guarantee correct versioning, it can ensure that versioning is possible for the programmer. With this support in place, a developer can guarantee that as his class library evolves, it will retain binary compatibility with existing client applications.

Compatible

C# does not live in a closed world. It allows you access to different APIs, with the foremost being the NGWS Common Language Specification (CLS). The CLS defines a standard for interoperation between languages that adhere to this standard. To enforce CLS compliance, the compiler of C# checks that all publicly exported entities comply, and raises an error if they do not.

Of course, you also want to be able to access your older COM objects. The NGWS runtime provides transparent access to COM. Integration with legacy code is presented in Chapter 10, "Interoperating with Unmanaged Code."

OLE Automation is a special kind of animal. Anyone who ever created an OLE Automation project in C++ will have come to love the various Automation data types. The good news is that C# supports them, without bothering you with details.

Finally, C# enables you to interoperate with C-style APIs. Any entry point in a DLL—given its C-styledness—is accessible from your applications. This feature for accessing native APIs is called Platform Invocation Services (PInvoke), and Chapter 10 shows a few examples of interoperating with C APIs.

Flexible

The last paragraph of the previous section might have raised an alert with C programmers. You might ask, "Aren't there APIs to which I have to pass a pointer?" You are right. There are not only a few such APIs, but quite a large number (a small understatement). This access to native WIN32 code sometimes makes using unsafe classic pointers mandatory (although some of it can be handled by the support of COM and PInvoke).

Although the default for C# code is safe mode, you can declare certain classes or only methods of classes to be unsafe. This declaration enables you to use pointers, structs, and statically allocated arrays. Both safe code and unsafe code run in the managed space, which implies that no marshaling is incurred when calling unsafe code from safe code.

What are the implications of dealing with your own memory in unsafe mode? Well, the garbage collector, of course, may not touch your memory locations and move them just as it does for managed code. Unsafe variables are pinned into the memory block managed by the garbage collector.

Summary

The C# language is derived from C and C++, and it was created for the enterprise developer who is willing to sacrifice a bit of C++'s raw power for more convenience and productivity. C# is modern, simple, object-oriented, and type-safe. It borrows a lot from C and C++, but it is considerably different in specific areas such as namespaces, classes, methods, and exception handling.

C# provides you with convenient features such as garbage collection, type safety, versioning, and more. The only "expense" is that by default your code operates in safe mode, where no pointers are allowed. Type safety pays off. However, if you need pointers, you can still use them via unsafe code—and no marshaling is involved when calling the unsafe code.

CHAPTER 2

The Underpinnings—
The NGWS Runtime

- The NGWS Runtime
- The Virtual Object System

Now that you have the big picture of C#, I want to give you the big picture of the NGWS runtime. C# depends on the runtime provided by NGWS; therefore, it is good to know how that runtime works, and what concepts are behind it.

The chapter, therefore, is split into two parts—everyday implications and use and the foundations. There is some overlap between both sections, but it helps to reinforce the concepts you are learning.

The NGWS Runtime

You are provided with a runtime environment by NGWS, the NGWS runtime. This runtime manages the execution of code, and it provides services that make programming easier. As long as the compiler that you use supports this runtime, you will benefit from this managed execution environment.

Your guess—that the C# compiler supports the NGWS runtime —is correct. However, it is not the only compiler that supports the NGWS runtime; Visual Basic and C++ do so also. The code that these compilers generate for NGWS runtime support is called *managed code*. The benefits your applications gains from the NGWS runtime are

- Cross-language integration (through the Common Language Specification)

- Automatic memory management (garbage collection)

- Cross-language exception handling (unified unwinding)

- Enhanced security (including type safety)

- Versioning support (the end of "DLL hell")

- Simplified model for component interaction

For the NGWS runtime to provide all these benefits, the compiler must emit metadata along with the managed code. The metadata describes the types in your code, and is stored along with your code (in the same PE— portable executable—file).

As you can see from the many cross-language features, the NGWS runtime is mainly about tight integration across multiple different programming languages. This support goes as far as allowing you to derive a C# class from a Visual Basic object (given that certain prereq- uisites that I'll discuss later are met).

One feature that C# programmers will like is that they don't have to worry about memory management—namely the all-famous memory leaks. The NGWS runtime provides the memory management, and the garbage collector releases the objects or variables when their lifetimes are over—when they are no longer referenced. I really like this feature because memory management in COM was my personal bane.

There are even bonuses when deploying a managed application or component. Because managed applications contain metadata, the NGWS runtime can use this information to ensure that your application has the specified versions of everything it needs. The net result is that your code is less likely to break because some dependency is not met. Another advantage of the metadata approach is that type information resides in the same file where the code resides—no more problems with the Registry!

The remainder of this section is split into two parts, each of which discusses various aspects of the NGWS runtime until your C# application is executed:

- Intermediate Language (IL) and metadata
- JITters

Intermediate Language and Metadata

The managed code generated by the C# compiler is not native code, but is Intermediate Language (IL) code. This IL code itself becomes the input for the managed execution process of the NGWS runtime. The ultimate advantage of IL code is that it is CPU independent; however, that means you need a compiler on the target machine to turn the IL code into native code.

The IL is generated by the compiler, but it is not the only thing that is provided for the runtime by the compiler. The compiler also generates metadata about your code, which tells the runtime more about your code, such as the definition of each type, and the signatures of each type's member as well as other data. Basically, metadata is what type libraries, Registry entries, and other information are for COM—however, the metadata is packaged directly with the executable code, not in disparate locations.

The IL and the metadata are placed in files that extend the PE format used for `.exe` and `.dll` files. When such a PE file is loaded, the runtime locates and extracts the metadata and IL from it.

Before moving on, I want to give you a very brief rundown of the categories of IL instructions that exist. Although this is not meant to be a complete list, nor do you need to learn it by heart to understand, it gives you a necessary insight into the foundation on which your C# programs depend:

- Arithmetic and logical operations

- Control flow

- Direct memory access

- Stack manipulation

- Argument and local variables

- Stack allocation

- Object model

- Values of instantiable types

- Critical region

- Arrays

- Typed locations

JITters

The managed code generated by C#—and other compilers capable of generating managed code—is IL code. Although the IL code is packaged in a valid PE file, you cannot execute it unless it is converted to managed native code. That is where the NGWS runtime JIT Just-in-Time (JIT) compilers—which are also referred to as JITters—come into the picture.

Why would you bother compiling code just-in-time? Why not take the whole IL PE file and compile it to native code? The answer is time—the time that is necessary to compile the IL code to CPU-specific code. It is much more efficient to compile as you go because some code pieces might never be executed—for example, in my word processor, the mail merge feature would never be compiled.

Technically speaking, the whole process works like this: When a type is loaded, the loader creates and attaches a stub to each method of the type. When a method is called for the first time, the stub passes control to the JIT. The JIT compiles the IL to native code, and changes the stub to point to the cached native code. Subsequent calls will execute the native code. At some point, all IL is converted to native code, and the JITter sits idle.

As I mentioned earlier, there is no single JIT compiler, but there are multiple ones. On Windows platforms, NGWS runtime ships with three different JITters:

- JIT—This is the default JIT compiler used by the NGWS runtime. It is an optimizing compiler back end, which performs a data flow analysis up front and creates highly optimized, managed native code as output. The JIT can cope with unrestricted sets of IL instructions; however, the resource requirements are quite considerable. The main constraints are the memory footprint, the resulting working set, and the time it takes to perform the optimizations.

- EconoJIT—In contrast to the main JIT, EconoJIT is targeted at high-speed conversion of IL to managed native code. It allows for caching of the generated native code; however, the output code isn't as optimized as the code produced by the main JIT. The advantage of fast code generation strategy pays off when memory is constrained—you can fit even large IL programs into this code cache by permanently discarding unused jitted code. Because JITting is fast, execution speed is still rather high.

- PreJIT—The PreJIT operates much more like a traditional compiler, although it is based on the main JIT compiler. It runs when an NGWS component is installed, and compiles the IL code to managed native code. The end results are, of course, faster loading time and faster application start time. (No more JITting is necessary.)

Two of the listed JITters are runtime JITters. However, how can you determine which JIT is to be used, and how it uses memory? There is a small utility named the JIT Compiler Manager (jitman.exe), which resides in the bin folder of the NGWS SDK installation folder. When executing the program, it adds an icon to the system tray—double-clicking that icon opens the program's dialog box (see Figure 2.1).

Figure 2.1

The JIT Compiler Manager enables you to set various performance-related options.

Although it is a small dialog box, the options you can choose in it are quite powerful. Each of the options is described in the following list:

- Use EconoJIT only—When this option is unchecked, the NGWS runtime uses the regular JIT compiler by default. The differences between the two JITters are explained earlier in this section.

- Max Code Pitch Overhead (%)—This setting pertains only to EconoJIT. It controls the percentage of time spent JITting versus executing code. If the threshold is exceeded, the code cache is expanded to reduce the amount of time spent JITting.

- Limit Size of Code Cache—This setting is unchecked by default. Not checking this option means that the cache will use as much memory as it can get. If you want to limit the cache size, enable this option, which allows you to use the Max Size of Cache (bytes) option.

- Max Size of Cache (bytes)—Controls the maximum size of the buffer that holds JITted code. Although you can very strictly limit this size, you should take care that the largest method fits this cache because otherwise the JIT compilation for this method will fail!

- Optimize For Size—Tells the JIT compiler to go for smaller code instead of faster code. By default, this setting is turned off.

- Enable Concurrent GC [garbage collection]—By default, garbage collection runs on the thread on which the user code runs. That means when GC happens, a slight delay in responsiveness might be noticeable. To prevent this from happening, turn on concurrent GC. Notice that concurrent garbage collection is slower than standard GC, and that it is available only on Windows 2000 at the time of this writing.

You can experiment with the different settings when creating projects with C#. When creating UI-intensive applications, you'll see the biggest difference by enabling concurrent GC.

The Virtual Object System

So far, you have seen only how the NGWS runtime works, but not the technical background of how it works and why it works the way it does. This section is all about the NGWS Virtual Object System (VOS).

The rules the NGWS runtime follow when declaring, using, and managing types are modeled in the Virtual Object System (VOS). The idea behind the VOS is to establish a framework that allows cross-language integration and type safety, without sacrificing performance when executing code.

The framework I mentioned is the foundation of the runtime's architecture. To help you better understand it, I will outline four areas that are important to know about when developing C# applications and components:

- The VOS type system—Provides a rich type system that is intended to support the complete implementation of a wide range of programming languages.

- Metadata—Describes and references the types defined by the VOS type system. The persistence format of metadata is independent of the programming language; therefore, metadata lends itself as an interchange mechanism for use between tools as well as with the Virtual Execution System of NGWS.

- The Common Language Specification (CLS)—The CLS defines a subset of types found in the VOS, as well as usage conventions. If a class library abides by the rules of the CLS, it is guaranteed that the class library can be used in all other programming languages that implement the CLS.

- The Virtual Execution System (VES)—This is the actual real-life implementation of the VOS. The VES is responsible for loading and executing programs that were written for the NGWS runtime.

Together, these four parts comprise the NGWS runtime architecture. Each of these parts is described at length in the following sections.

The VOS Type System

The VOS type system provides a rich type system that is intended to support the complete implementation of a wide range of programming languages. Therefore, the VOS has to support object-oriented languages as well as procedural programming languages.

Today, there are many similar—but subtly incompatible—types around. Consider the integer data type, for example: In VB, it is 16 bits in length, whereas in C++, it is 32 bits. There are many more examples, especially the data types used for date and time, and database types. This incompatibility unnecessarily complicates the creation and maintenance of distributed applications, especially when multiple programming languages are involved.

Another problem is that because of the subtle differences in programming languages, you cannot reuse a type created in one language in a different one. (COM partially solves this with the binary standard of interfaces.) Code reuse is definitely limited today.

The biggest hurdle for distributed applications is that the object models of the various programming languages are not uniform. Almost everything differs: events, properties, persistence—you name it.

The VOS is here to change that picture. The VOS defines types that describe values and specify a contract that all values of the type must support. Because of the aforementioned support for object-oriented (OO) and procedural programming languages, two kinds of entities exist: values and objects.

For a value, the type describes the storage representation as well as operations that can be performed on it. Objects are more powerful because the type is explicitly stored in its representation. Each object has an identity that distinguishes it from all other objects. The different VOS types supported by C# are presented in Chapter 4, "C# Types."

Metadata

Although metadata is used to describe and reference the types defined by the VOS type system, it is not exclusively locked to this single purpose. When you write a program, the types you declare—be they value types or reference types—are introduced to the NGWS runtime type system by using type declarations, which are described in the metadata stored inside the PE executable.

Basically, metadata is used for various tasks: To represent the information that the NGWS runtime uses to locate and load classes, to lay out instances of these classes in memory, to resolve method invocations, to translate IL to native code, to enforce security, and to set up runtime context boundaries.

You do not have to care about the generation of the metadata. Metadata generation is done for you by C#'s code-to-IL compiler (not the JIT compiler). The code-to-IL compiler emits the binary metadata information into the PE file for you, and it does so in a standardized way—not like C++ compilers that create their own decorated names for exported functions.

The main advantage you gain from combining the metadata with the executable code is that the information about the types is persisted along with the type itself, and it is no longer spread across multiple locations. It also helps to address versioning problems that exist in COM. Furthermore, in NGWS runtime, you can use different versions of a library in the same context because the libraries are referenced not by the Registry, but by the metadata contained in the executable code.

The Common Language Specification

The Common Language Specification is not exactly a part of the Virtual Object System—it is a specialization. The CLS defines a subset of types found in the VOS, as well as usage conventions that must be followed to be CLS-compliant.

So, what is this fuss all about? If a class library abides by the rules of CLS, it is guaranteed to be usable by clients of other programming languages that also adhere to the CLS. CLS is about language interoperability. Therefore, the conventions must be followed only on the externally visible items such as methods, properties, events, and so on.

The advantage of what I have described is that you can do the following: Write a component in C#, derive from it in Visual Basic and, because the functionality added in VB is so great, derive again from the VB class in C#. This works as long as all the externally visible (accessible) items abide by the rules of CLS.

The code I present in this book does not care about CLS compliance. However, you should care about CLS compliance when building your class library. Therefore, I have provided Table 2.1 to define the compliance rules for types and items that might be externally visible.

This list is not complete—it contains only some of the most-important items. I don't point out the CLS compliance of every type presented in this book, so it is a good idea to at least glance over the table to see which functionality is available when you are hunting for CLS compliance. Don't worry if you are not familiar with every term in this table—you will learn about these terms during the course of this book.

Table 2.1 Types and Features in the Common Language Specification

Primitive Types

```
bool
```
```
char
```
```
byte
```
```
short
```
```
int
```
```
long
```
```
float
```
```
double
```
```
string
```
`object` (The mother of all objects)

Arrays

The dimension must be known (>=1), and the lower bound must be zero.

Element type must be a CLS type.

Types

Can be abstract or sealed.

Zero or more interfaces can be implemented. Different interfaces are allowed to have methods with the same name and signature.

A type can be derived from exactly one type. Member overriding and hiding are allowed.

Can have zero or more members, which are fields, methods, events, or types.

The type can have zero or more constructors.

The visibility of the type can be public or local to the NGWS component; however, only public members are considered part of the interface of the type.

All value types must inherit from `System.ValueType`. The exception is an enumeration—it must inherit from `System.Enum`.

continues

Table 2.1   continued

Type Members

Type members are allowed to hide or override other members in another type.

The types of both the arguments and return values must be CLS-compliant types.

Constructors, methods, and properties can be overloaded.

A type can have abstract members, but only as long as the type is not sealed.

Methods

A method can be either static, virtual, or instance.

Virtual and instance methods can be abstract or have an implementation. Static methods must always have an implementation.

Virtual methods can be final (or not).

Fields

Can be static or nonstatic.

Static fields can be literal or initialize-only.

Properties

Can be exposed as `get` and `set` methods instead of using property syntax.

The return type of `get` and the first argument of the `set` method must be the same CLS type—the type of the property.

Properties must differ by name; a different property type is not sufficient for differentiation.

Because property access is implemented with methods, you cannot implement methods named `get_PropertyName` and `set_PropertyName` if `PropertyName` is a property defined in the same class.

Properties can be indexed.

Property accessors must follow this naming pattern: `get_PropName`, `set_PropName`.

Enumerations

Underlying type must be `byte`, `short`, `int`, or `long`.

Each member is a static literal field of the enum's type.

An enumeration cannot implement any interfaces.

You are allowed to assign the same value to multiple fields.

An enumeration must inherit from `System.Enum` (performed implicitly in C#).

Exceptions

Can be thrown and caught.

Self-programmed exceptions must inherit from `System.Exception`.

Interfaces

Can require implementation of other interfaces.

An interface can define properties, events, and virtual methods. The implementation is up to the deriving class.

Events

Add and remove methods must be either both provided or both absent. Each of these methods takes one parameter, which is a class derived from `System.Delegate`.

Must following this naming pattern: add_*EventName*, remove_*EventName*, and raise_*EventName*.

Custom Attributes

Can use only the following types: `Type`, `string`, `char`, `bool`, `byte`, `short`, `int`, `long`, `float`, `double`, enum (of a CLS type), and `object`.

Delegates

Can be created and invoked.

Identifiers

An identifier's first character must come from a restricted set.

It is not possible to distinguish two or more identifiers solely by case in a single scope (no case sensitivity).

The Virtual Execution System

The Virtual Execution System implements the Virtual Object System. The VES is created by implementing an execution engine (EE) that is responsible for the runtime of NGWS. This execution engine executes your applications that were written and compiled in C#.

The following components are part of the VES:

- The Intermediate Language (IL)—It is designed to be easily targeted by a wide range of compilers. Out of the box, you get C++, Visual Basic, and C# compilers that are capable of generating IL.

- Loading managed code—This includes resolving names, laying out classes in memory, and creating the stubs that are necessary for the JIT compilation. The class loader also enforces security by performing consistency checks, including the enforcement of certain accessibility rules.

- Conversion of IL to native code via JIT—The IL code is not designed as a traditional interpreted bytecode or tree code. IL conversion is really a compilation.

- Loading metadata, checking type safety, and integrity of the methods.

- Garbage collection (GC) and exception handling—Both are services based on the stack format. Managed code enables you to trace the stack at runtime. For the runtime to understand the individual stack frames, a code manager has to be provided either by the JITter or the compiler.

- Profiling and debugging services—Both of these depend on information produced by the source language compiler. Two maps must be emitted: a map from source language constructs to addresses in the instruction stream, and a map from addresses to locations in the stack frame. These maps are recomputed when conversion from IL to native code is performed.

- Management of threads and contexts, as well as remoting—The VES provides these services to managed code.

The list provided is not complete, but it is enough for you to understand how the runtime is backed by the infrastructure provided by the VES. There certainly will be books dedicated completely to the NGWS runtime, and those books will drill deeper into each topic.

Summary

In this chapter, I took you on a tour of the NGWS runtime. I described how it works for you when creating, compiling, and deploying C# programs. You learned about the Intermediate Language (IL), and how metadata is used to describe the types that are compiled to IL. Both metadata and IL are used by JITters to examine and execute your code. You can even choose which JITters to use to execute your application.

The second part of this chapter dealt with the theory of why the runtime behaves the way it does. You learned about the Virtual Object System (VOS), and the parts that comprise it. Most interesting for class library designers is the Common Language Specification (CLS), which sets up rules for language interoperation based on the VOS. Finally, you saw how the Virtual Execution System (VES) is an implementation of the VOS by the NGWS runtime.

CHAPTER 3

Your First C# Application

- Choosing an Editor
- The Hello World Code
- Compiling the Application
- Input and Output
- Adding Comments

Keeping with the tradition of programming books, I'll start presenting C# with the famous Hello World program. This chapter is short because its intention is to show you the basic building blocks of a C# application, how to write and compile the application, as well as the input and output code that is used throughout this book in the examples.

Choosing an Editor

Although I am a hardcore Notepad fanatic, I don't recommend it this time for editing C# source files. The reason is that you are dealing with a real programming language, one with a compiler that can produce a rather large number of error messages. (C++ programmers know what I am talking about.)

You have several choices for an editor. You could reconfigure your trusty old Visual C++ 6.0 to work with C# source files. A second option is to work with the new Visual Studio 7. Third, you can use any third-party programmer's editor, preferably one that supports line numbers, color coding, tool integration (for the compiler), and a good search function. One example of such a tool is CodeWright, which is shown in Figure 3.1.

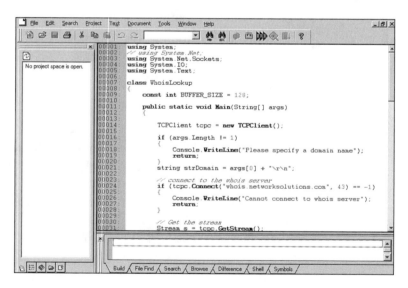

Figure 3.1

CodeWright is one of many possible editors you can use for creating C# code files.

Of course, none of the mentioned editors is mandatory to create a C# program—Notepad will definitely do. However, if you are considering writing larger projects, it is a good idea to switch.

The Hello World Code

After this short detour about editors, let's get back to the most famous little application. The shortest C# version of this application can be seen in Listing 3.1. Save it to a file named `helloworld.cs` so that you can follow the remaining steps, such as compiling the application.

Listing 3.1 The Hello World Program at Its Simplest

```
1: class HelloWorld
2: {
3:   public static void Main()
4:   {
5:     System.Console.WriteLine("Hello World");
6:   }
7: }
```

In C#, code blocks (statements) are enclosed by braces (`{` and `}`). Therefore, even if you don't have prior experience in C++, you can tell that the `Main()` method is part of the `HelloWorld` class statement because it is enclosed in the angle brackets of its definition.

The entry point to a C# application (executable) is the static `Main` method, which must be contained in a class. There can be only one class defined with this signature, unless you advise the compiler which `Main` method it should use (otherwise, a compiler error is generated).

In contrast to C++, `Main` has a capital M, not the lowercase you are already used to. In this method, your program starts and ends. You can call other methods—as in this example, for text output—or create objects and invoke methods on those.

As you can see, the `Main` method has a `void` return type:

```
public static void Main()
```

Although C++ programmers definitely feel at home looking at these statements, programmers of other languages might not. First, the `public` access modifier tells us that this method is accessible by everyone—which is a prerequisite for it to be called. Next, `static` means that the method can be called without creating an instance of the class first—all you have to do is call it with the class's name:

```
HelloWorld.Main();
```

However, I do not recommend executing this code in the Main method. Recursions cause stack overflows.

Another important aspect is the return type. For the method Main, you have a choice of either void (which means no return value at all), or int for an integer result (the error level returned by an application). Therefore, two possible Main methods look like

```
public static void Main()
public static int Main()
```

C++ programmers will also know what I am presenting next—the command-line parameters array that can be passed to an application. This looks like

```
public static void Main(string[] args)
```

I won't elaborate now on how to access the parameters, but I want to give C++ programmers an upfront warning: In contrast to C++, the application path is not part of this array. Only the parameters are contained in this array.

After this not-so-short introduction to the Main method, let's move on to the only real line of code—the one that prints "Hello World" to the screen:

```
System.Console.WriteLine("Hello World");
```

If it weren't for the System part, one would immediately be able to guess that WriteLine is a static method of the Console object. So what does this System stand for? It is the namespace (scope) in which the Console object is contained. Because it's not really practical to prefix the Console object with this namespace part every time, you can import the namespace in your application as shown in Listing 3.2.

Listing 3.2   Importing the Namespace in Your Application

```
1: using System;
2:
3: class HelloWorld
4: {
5:   public static void Main()
6:   {
7:     Console.WriteLine("Hello World");
8:   }
9: }
```

All you have to do is add a using directive for the System namespace. From then on, you can use elements of that namespace without having to qualify them. There are many namespaces in the NGWS framework, and we will explore only a few objects from this huge pool. However, Chapter 8, "Writing Components in C#," will introduce you to creating your own namespaces for your objects.

Compiling the Application

Because the NGWS runtime ships with all compilers (VB, C++, and C#), you do not need to buy a separate development tool to compile your application to IL (intermediate language). However, if you have never compiled an application using a command-line compiler (and know makefiles only by name and not by heart), this will be a first for you.

Open a command prompt and switch to the directory in which you saved helloworld.cs. Issue the following command:

```
csc helloworld.cs
```

helloworld.cs is compiled and linked to helloworld.exe. Because the source code is error-free (of course!), the C# compiler does not complain and, as shown in Figure 3.2, completes without hiccup.

Figure 3.2

Compile your application using the command-line compiler `csc.exe`.

Now you are ready to run your very first application written in C#. Simply issue `helloworld` at the command prompt. The output generated is `"Hello World"`.

Before moving on, I want to get a little bit fancy about your first application and use a compiler switch:

```
csc /out:hello.exe helloworld.cs
```

This switch tells the compiler that the output file is to be named `hello.exe`. It's really not a big deal, but it is an apprentice piece for future compiler use in this book.

Input and Output

So far, I demonstrated only simple constant string output to the console. Although this book introduces concepts of C# programming and not user-interface programming, I need to get you up to speed on some simple console input and output methods—the C equivalents of `scanf` and `printf`, or the C++ equivalents of `cin` and `cout`. I cannot offer an equivalent for VB because console access wasn't part of the core language.

You need only to be able to read user input and present some information to the user. Listing 3.3 shows how to read a requested name input from the user, and print a customized "Hello" message.

Listing 3.3   Reading Input from the Console

```
 1: using System;
 2:
 3: class InputOutput
 4: {
 5:   public static void Main()
 6:   {
 7:     Console.Write("Please enter your name: ");
 8:     string strName = Console.ReadLine();
 9:     Console.WriteLine("Hello " + strName);
10:   }
11: }
```

Line 7 uses a new method of the Console object for presenting textual information to the user: the Write method. Its only difference from the WriteLine method is that Write does not add a line break to the output. I used this approach so that the user can enter the name on the same line as the question.

After the user enters his name (and presses the Enter key), the input is read into a string variable using the ReadLine method. The name string is concatenated with the "Hello " constant string and presented to the user with the already familiar WriteLine method (see Figure 3.3).

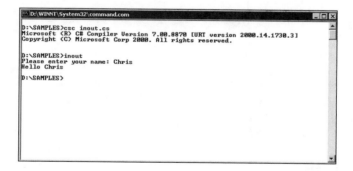

Figure 3.3

Compiling and running the customized Hello application.

You are almost finished with learning the necessary input and output functionality of the NGWS framework. However, you need one thing for presenting multiple values to the user: writing out a formatted string to the user. One example is shown in Listing 3.4.

Listing 3.4   Using a Different Output Method

```
 1: using System;
 2:
 3: class InputOutput
 4: {
 5:   public static void Main()
 6:   {
 7:      Console.Write("Please enter your name: ");
 8:      string strName = Console.ReadLine();
 9:      Console.WriteLine("Hello {0}",strName);
10:   }
11: }
```

Line 9 contains a `Console.WriteLine` statement that uses a formatted string. The format string in this example is

```
"Hello {0}"
```

The `{0}` is replaced for the first variable following the format string in the argument list of the `WriteLine` method. You can format up to three variables using this technique:

```
Console.WriteLine("Hello {0} {1}, from {2}",
➥strFirstname, strLastname, strCity);
```

Of course, you are not limited to supplying only string variables. You can supply any type, and types are discussed at length in Chapter 4, "C# Types."

Adding Comments

When writing code, you should also write comments to accompany that code—with notes about implementation details, change history, and so on. Although what information (if any) you provide in comments is up to you, you must stick to C#'s way of writing comments. Listing 3.5 shows the two different approaches you can take.

Listing 3.5   Adding Comments to Your Code

```
 1: using System;
 2:
 3: class HelloWorld
 4: {
 5:   public static void Main()
 6:   {
 7:      // this is a single-line comment
 8:      /* this comment spans
 9:      multiple lines */
10:      Console.WriteLine(/*"Hello World"*/);
11:   }
12: }
```

The // characters denote a single-line comment. You can use // on a line of their own, or they can follow a code statement:

```
int nMyVar = 10;   // blah blah
```

Everything after the // on a line is considered a comment; therefore, you can also use them to comment out an entire line or part of a line of source code. This is the same kind of comment introduced in C++.

If you want a comment to span multiple lines, you must use the /* */ combination of characters. This type of comment is available in C, and is also available in C++ and C# in addition to single-line comments. Because C/C++ and C# share this multiline comment type, they also share the same caveat. Look at the following line of code:

```
/* Console.WriteLine("Hello World"); */
```

I simply commented out the entire line using /* */. Now I assume that this line is part of a larger piece of code, and I decide that I want to temporarily disable the entire block:

```
/*
...
/* Console.WriteLine("Hello World"); */
...
*/
```

The problem with this construct is that the */ in the "Hello World" line closes the /* of the first line. The remainder of the code is available to the compiler, and you will see some interesting error messages. At least the last `*/` is flagged as an easily attributable error. I just wanted to raise your awareness about such errors.

Summary

In this chapter, you created, compiled, and executed your first C# application: the famous "Hello World" application. I used this sweet little application to introduce you to the `Main` method, which is an application's entry point—and also its exit point. This method can return either no result or an integer error level. If your application is called with parameters, you can—but need not—read and use them.

After compiling and testing the application, you learned more about the input and output methods that are provided by the `Console` object. They are just enough to create meaningful console examples for learning C#, however, most of your user interface will be WFC, WinForms, or ASP+.

CHAPTER 4

C# Types

- Value Types
- Reference Types
- Boxing and Unboxing

Now that you know how to build a simple C# program, I'm introducing you to the type system of C#. In this chapter, you learn how to use the different value and reference types, and what the boxing and unboxing mechanism can do for you. Although this chapter isn't heavy on examples, you learn a lot of important information about how to build a program that gains most from the provided types.

Value Types

A variable of a certain value type always contains a value of that type. C# forces you to initialize variables before you use them in a calculation— no more problems with uninitialized variables because the compiler will tell you when you try to use them.

When assigning a value to a value type, the value is actually copied. In contrast, for reference types, only the reference is copied; the actual value remains at the same memory location, but now two objects point to it (reference it).

The value types of C# can be grouped as follows:

- Simple types
- `struct` types
- Enumeration types

Simple Types

The simple types that are present in C# share some characteristics. First, they are all aliases of the NGWS system types. Second, constant expressions consisting of simple types are evaluated only at compilation time, not at runtime. Last, simple types can be initialized with literals.

The simple types of C# are grouped as follows:

- Integral types
- `bool` type
- `char` type (special case of integral type)
- Floating-point types
- The `decimal` type

Integral Types

There are nine integral types in C#: `sbyte`, `byte`, `short`, `ushort`, `int`, `uint`, `long`, `ulong`, and `char` (discussed in a section of its own). They have the following characteristics:

- The `sbyte` type represents signed 8-bit integers with values between −128 and 127.

- The `byte` type represents unsigned 8-bit integers with values between 0 and 255.

- The `short` type represents signed 16-bit integers with values between −32,768 and 32,767.

- The `ushort` type represents unsigned 16-bit integers with values between 0 and 65,535.

- The `int` type represents signed 32-bit integers with values between −2,147,483,648 and 2,147,483,647.

- The `uint` type represents unsigned 32-bit integers with values between 0 and 4,294,967,295.

- The `long` type represents signed 64-bit integers with values between −9,223,372,036,854,775,808 and 9,223,372,036,854,775,807.

- The `ulong` type represents unsigned 64-bit integers with values between 0 and 18,446,744,073,709,551,615.

Both VB and C programmers might be surprised by the new ranges represented by the `int` and `long` data types. In contrast to other programming languages, in C#, `int` is no longer dependent on the size of a machine word and `long` is set to 64-bit.

bool Type

The `bool` data type represents the Boolean values true and false. You can assign either true or false to a Boolean variable, or you can assign an expression that evaluates to either value:

```
bool bTest = (80 > 90);
```

In contrast to C and C++, in C#, the value true is no longer represented by any nonzero value. There is no conversion between other integral types to bool to enforce this convention.

char Type

The char type represents a single Unicode character. A Unicode character is 16 bits in length, and it can be used to represent most of the languages in the world. You can assign a character to a char variable as follows:

```
char chSomeChar = 'A';
```

In addition, you can assign a char variable via a hexadecimal escape sequence (prefix \x) or Unicode representation (prefix \u):

```
char chSomeChar = '\x0065';
```

```
char chSomeChar = '\u0065';
```

There are no implicit conversions from char to other data types available. That means treating a char variable just as another integral data type is not possible in C#—this is another area where C programmers have to change habits. However, you can perform an explicit cast:

```
char chSomeChar = (char)65;
int nSomeInt = (int)'A';
```

There are still the escape sequences (character literals) that there are in C. To refresh your memory, take a look at Table 4.1.

Table 4.1   Escape Sequences

Escape Sequence	Character Name
\'	Single quotation mark
\"	Double quotation mark
\\	Backslash
\0	Null
\a	Alert
\b	Backspace
\f	Form feed
\n	New line

Escape Sequence	Character Name
\r	Carriage return
\t	Horizontal tab
\v	Vertical tab

Floating-Point Types

Two data types are referred to as floating-point types: `float` and `double`. They differ in range and precision:

- `float`: The range is 1.5×10^{-45} to 3.4×10^{38} with a precision of 7 digits.

- `double`: The range is 5.0×10^{-324} to 1.7×10^{308} with a precision of 15–16 digits.

When performing calculations with either of the floating-point types, the following values can be produced:

- Positive and negative zero

- Positive and negative infinity

- Not-a-Number value (NaN)

- The finite set of nonzero values

Another rule for calculations is that if one of the types in an expression is a floating-point type, all other types are converted to the floating-point type before the calculation is performed.

The *decimal* Type

The `decimal` type is a high-precision, 128-bit data type that is intended to be used for financial and monetary calculations. It can represent values ranging from approximately 1.0×10^{-28} to 7.9×10^{28} with 28 to 29 significant digits. It is important to note that the precision is given in digits, not decimal places. Operations are exact to a maximum of 28 decimal places.

As you can see, the range is narrower as for the `double` data type, however, it is much more precise. Therefore, no implicit conversions exist between `decimal` and `double`—in one direction you might generate an overflow; in the other you might lose precision. You have to explicitly request conversion with a cast.

When defining a variable and assigning a value to it, use the `m` suffix to denote that it is a `decimal` value:

```
decimal decMyValue = 1.0m;
```

If you omit the `m`, the variable will be treated as `double` by the compiler before it is assigned.

struct Types

A `struct` type can declare constructors, constants, fields, methods, properties, indexers, operators, and nested types. Although the features I list here look like a full-blown class, the difference between `struct` and `class` in C# is that `struct` is a value type and `class` is a reference type. This is in contrast to C++, where you can define a class by using the `struct` keyword.

The main idea of using `struct` is to create lightweight objects, such as Point, FileInfo, and so on. You conserve memory because no additional references are created as are needed for class objects. For instance, when declaring arrays containing thousands of objects, this makes quite a difference.

Listing 4.1 contains a simple `struct` named IP, which represents an IP address using four fields of type `byte`. I did not include methods and the like because these work just as with classes, which are described in detail in the next chapter.

Listing 4.1   Defining a Simple `struct`

```
1: using System;
2:
3: struct IP
4: {
5:   public byte b1,b2,b3,b4;
6: }
```

```
 7:
 8: class Test
 9: {
10:   public static void Main()
11:   {
12:     IP myIP;
13:     myIP.b1 = 192;
14:     myIP.b2 = 168;
15:     myIP.b3 = 1;
16:     myIP.b4 = 101;
17:     Console.Write("{0}.{1}.",myIP.b1,myIP.b2);
18:     Console.Write("{0}.{1}",myIP.b3,myIP.b4);
19:   }
20: }
```

Enumeration Types

When you want to declare a distinct type consisting of a set of named constants, the enum type is what you are looking for. In its most simple form, it can look like this:

```
enum MonthNames { January, February, March, April };
```

Because I stuck with the defaults, the enumeration elements are of type int, and the first element has the value 0. Each successive element is increased by one. If you want to assign an explicit value for the first element, you can do so by setting it to 1:

```
enum MonthNames { January=1, February, March, April };
```

If you want to assign arbitrary values to every element—even duplicate values—this is no problem either:

```
enum MonthNames { January=31, February=28, March=31, April=30 };
```

The final choice is a data type different from int. You can assign it in a statement like this:

```
enum MonthNames : byte { January=31, February=28, March=31, April=30 };
```

The types you can use are limited to long, int, short, and byte.

Reference Types

In contrast to value types, reference types do not store the actual data they represent, but they store references to the actual data. The following reference types are present in C# for you to use:

- The object type
- The class type
- Interfaces
- Delegates
- The string type
- Arrays

The *object* Type

The object type is the mother of all types—it is the ultimate base class of all other types. Because it is the base class for all objects, you can assign values of any type to it. For example, an integer:

```
object theObj = 123;
```

A warning to all C++ programmers: object is not the equivalent to void* that you might be looking for. It is a good idea to forget about pointers anyway.

The object type is used when a value type is *boxed* (made available as an object). Boxing and unboxing are discussed later in this chapter.

The *class* Type

A class type can contain data members, function members, and nested types. Data members are constants, fields, and events. Function members include methods, properties, indexers, operators, constructors, and destructors. The functionality of class and struct are very similar; however, as stated earlier, structs are value types and classes are reference types.

In contrast to C++, only single inheritance is allowed. (You cannot have multiple base classes from which a new object derives.) However, a class in C# can derive from multiple interfaces, which are described in the next section.

Chapter 5, "Classes," is dedicated to programming with classes. This section is intended only to give an overview of where C# classes fit into the type picture.

Interfaces

An interface declares a reference type that has abstract members only. Similar concepts in C++ are members of a `struct`, and methods equal to zero. If you don't know any of those concepts, here is what an interface actually does in C#: Only the signature exists, but there is no implementation code at all. An implication of this is that you cannot instantiate an interface, only an object that derives from that interface.

You can define methods, properties, and indexers in an interface. So, what is so special about an interface as compared to a class? When defining a class, you can derive from multiple interfaces, whereas you can derive from only one class.

You might ask, "Okay, but I have to do all the implementation work for the interface's members, so what do I gain from this approach?" I want to take an example from the NGWS framework: Many classes implement the `IDictionary` interface. You can get access to that interface with a simple cast:

```
IDictionary myDict = (IDictionary)someobjectthatsupportsit;
```

Now your code can access the dictionary. But wait, I said many classes can implement this interface—therefore, you can reuse the code for accessing the `IDictionary` interface in multiple places! Learn once, use everywhere.

When you decide to use interfaces in your class design, it is a good idea to learn more about object-oriented design. This book cannot teach you those concepts. However, you can learn how to build the interface. The

following piece of code defines the interface IFace, which has a single
method:

```
interface IFace
{
  void ShowMyFace();
}
```

As I mentioned, you cannot instantiate an object from this definition, but
you can derive a class from it. However, that class must implement the
ShowMyFace abstract method:

```
class CFace:IFace
{
  public void ShowMyFace()
  {
    Console.WriteLine("implementation");
  }
}
```

The only difference between interface members and class members is
that interface members do not have an implementation. Therefore, I
won't duplicate information presented in the next chapter.

Delegates

A delegate encapsulates a method with a certain signature. Basically,
delegates are the type-safe and secure version of function pointers
(callback functionality). You can encapsulate both static and instance
methods in a delegate instance.

Although you can use delegates as is with methods, their main use is with
a class's events. Once again, I want to refer you to the next chapter,
where classes are discussed at length.

The *string* Type

C programmers might be surprised, but yes, C# has a base type string
for manipulating string data. The string class derives directly from
object, and it is sealed, which means that you cannot derive from it. Just
as with all other types, string is an alias for a predefined class:

```
System.String.
```

Its usage is very simple:

```
string myString = "some text";
```

Concatenation of strings is easy, too:

```
string myString = "some text" + " and a bit more";
```

And if you want to access a single character, all you need to do is access the indexer:

```
char chFirst = myString[0];
```

When you compare two strings for equality, you simply use the == comparison operator:

```
if (myString == yourString) ...
```

I just want to mention that although `string` is a reference type, the comparison it performs compares the values, not the references (memory addresses).

The `string` type is used in almost every example in this book, and in the course of these examples, I'll introduce you to some of the most interesting methods that are exposed by the `string` object.

Arrays

An array contains variables that are accessed through computed indices. All variables contained in an array—referred to as *elements*—must be of the same type. This type is then called the "type of the array." Arrays can store integer objects, string objects, or any type of object you can come up with.

The dimensions of an array are the so-called rank, which determines the number of indices associated with an array element. The most commonly used array is a single dimensional array (rank one). A multidimensional array has a rank greater than one. Each dimension's index starts at zero and runs to dimension length minus one.

That should be enough theory. Let's take a look at an array that is initialized with an array initializer:

```
string[] arrLanguages = { "C", "C++", "C#" };
```

This is, in effect, a shorthand for

```
arrLanguages[0]="C"; arrLanguages[1]="C++"; arrLanguages[2]="C#";
```

but the compiler does all the work for you. Of course, this would also work for multidimensional array initializers:

```
int[,] arr = {{0,1}, {2,3}, {4,5}};
```

This is just a shorthand for

```
arr[0,0] = 0; arr[0,1] = 1;
arr[1,0] = 2; arr[1,1] = 3;
arr[2,0] = 4; arr[2,1] = 5;
```

If you do not want to initialize an array upfront, but do know its size, the declaration looks like this:

```
int[,] myArr = new int[5,3];
```

If the size must be dynamically computed, the statement for array creation can be written as

```
int nVar = 5;
int[] arrToo = new int[nVar];
```

As I stated at the beginning of this section, you may stuff anything inside an array as long as all elements are of the same type. Therefore, if you want to put anything inside one array, declare its type to be object.

Boxing and Unboxing

I have presented various value types and reference types throughout the course of this chapter. For speed reasons, you would use value types—which are nothing more than memory blocks of a certain size. However, sometimes the convenience of objects is good to have for value types as well.

This is where boxing and unboxing, which are central concepts of C#'s type system, enter the stage. This mechanism forms the binding link between value types and reference types by permitting a value type to be converted to and from type object. Everything is ultimately an object—however, only when it needs to be.

Boxing Conversions

Boxing a value refers to implicitly converting any value type to the type object. When a value type is boxed, an object instance is allocated and the value of the value type is copied into the new object.

Look at the following example:

```
int nFunny = 2000;
object oFunny = nFunny;
```

The assignment in the second line implicitly invokes a boxing operation. The value of the nFunny integer variable is copied to the object oFunny. Now both the integer variable and the object variable exist on the stack, but the value of the object resides on the heap.

So, what does that imply? The values are independent of each other—there is no link between them. (oFunny does not reference the value of nFunny.) The following code illustrates the consequences:

```
int nFunny = 2000;
object oFunny = nFunny;
oFunny = 2001;
Console.WriteLine("{0} {1}", nFunny, oFunny);
```

When the code changes the value of oFunny, the value of nFunny is not changed. As long as you keep this copy behavior in mind, you'll be able to use the object functionality of value types to your greatest advantage!

Unboxing Conversions

In contrast to boxing, unboxing is an explicit operation—you have to tell the compiler which value type you want to extract from the object. When performing the unboxing operation, C# checks that the value type you request is actually stored in the object instance. Upon successful verification, the value is unboxed.

This is how unboxing is performed:

```
int nFunny = 2000;
object oFunny = nFunny;
int nNotSoFunny = (int)oFunny;
```

If you mistakenly requested a `double` value

```
double nNotSoFunny = (double)oFunny;
```

the NGWS runtime would raise an `InvalidCastException` exception. You can learn more about exception handling in Chapter 7, "Exception Handling."

Summary

In this chapter, you learned about the various types that are available in C#. The simple value types include integral, `bool`, `char`, floating-point, and `decimal`. These are the types you will use most often for mathematical and financial calculations, as well as for logical expressions.

Before diving into the reference types, I showed one look-alike to the class, the `struct` type. It behaves almost like a class, but it is a value type, which makes it more suitable for scenarios in which you need a large number of small objects.

The reference type section started with the mother of all objects, the `object` itself. It is the base class for all objects in C#, and it is also used for boxing and unboxing of value types. In addition, I took you on a tour of delegates, strings, and arrays.

The type that will most haunt you as C# programmer is the `class`. It is the heart of object-oriented programming in C#, and the next chapter is entirely dedicated to getting you up to speed with this exciting and powerful type.

CHAPTER 5

Classes

- Constructors and Destructors
- Methods
- Class Properties
- Indexers
- Events
- Applying Modifiers

The previous chapter discussed data types and their usage at length. Now we move on to the most important construct in C#—the class. Without a class, no single C# program would compile. This chapter assumes that you know the basic building blocks of a class: methods, properties, constructors, and destructors. C# adds to these with indexers as well as events.

In this chapter, you learn about the following class-related topics:

- Working with constructors and destructors

- Writing methods for classes

- Adding property accessors to a class

- Implementing indexers

- Creating events and subscribing clients to events via delegates

- Applying class, member, and access modifiers

Constructors and Destructors

The first statements that execute before you can access a class's methods, properties, or anything else are the ones contained in the constructor of the respective class. Even if you don't write a constructor yourself, a default constructor is provided for you:

```
class TestClass
{
  public TestClass(): base() {}  // provided by the compiler
}
```

A constructor always has the same name as the class; however, it does not have a return type declared. In general, constructors are always public, and you use them to initialize variables:

```
public TestClass()
{
  // initialization code here
  // for variables, etc.
}
```

If your class contains only static members (members that can be called on the type, not an instance), you can create a *private* constructor.

```
private TestClass() {}
```

Although access modifiers are discussed later in this chapter at more length, *private* means that the constructor isn't accessible from the outside of the class. Therefore, it cannot be called, and no object can be instantiated from the class definition.

You are not limited to a parameterless constructor—you can pass initial arguments to initialize certain members:

```
public TestClass(string strName, int nAge) { ... }
```

As a C/C++ programmer, you might be used to writing an additional method for initialization because no return values are available in constructors. Although there are, of course, no return values available in C# either, you could throw a custom exception to get back a result from the constructor. More information about exception handling is presented in Chapter 7, "Exception Handling."

There is, however, one method that you should consider writing when you hold references to expensive resources: a method that can be called explicitly to release all those resources. The question is why you should write an additional method, when you could do the same in the destructor (named with the prefix ~ and the class's name):

```
public ~TestClass()
{
  // clean up
}
```

The reason you should write an additional method is the garbage collector, which isn't invoked immediately after the variable goes out of scope, but only at certain intervals or memory conditions. It could happen that you lock the resource much longer than you intended. Therefore, it is a good idea to provide an explicit Release method, which can also be called from the destructor:

```
public void Release()
{
  // release all expensive resources
}

public ~TestClass()
{
  Release();
}
```

The invocation of the `Release` method in the destructor is not mandatory—the garbage collection would take care of releasing the objects anyway. But it is good practice not to forget to clean up.

Methods

Now that your object initializes and terminates properly, all that is left to do is to add functionality to your class. In most cases, the major part of functionality is implemented in methods. You have seen static methods in use already. However, those are part of the type (class), but not of the instance (object).

To get you started quickly, I have arranged the nagging questions about methods into three sections:

- Method parameters
- Overriding methods
- Method hiding

Method Parameters

For a method to process changing values, you somehow must pass the values into the method, and also get back results from the method. The following three sections deal with issues that arise from passing values in and getting results back to the caller:

- In parameters
- `ref` parameters
- `out` parameters

In Parameters

A parameter type you have seen already in examples is the in parameter. You use an in parameter to pass a variable by value to a method—the method's variable is initialized with a copy of the value from the caller. Listing 5.1 demonstrates the use of in parameters.

Listing 5.1   Passing Parameters by Value

```
 1: using System;
 2:
 3: public class SquareSample
 4: {
 5:   public int CalcSquare(int nSideLength)
 6:   {
 7:     return nSideLength*nSideLength;
 8:   }
 9: }
10:
11: class SquareApp
12: {
13:   public static void Main()
14:   {
15:     SquareSample sq = new SquareSample();
16:     Console.WriteLine(sq.CalcSquare(25).ToString());
17:   }
18: }
```

Because I pass the value and not a reference to a variable, I can use a constant expression (25) when I call the method (see line 16). The integer result is passed back to the caller as a return value, which is written to the console immediately without storing it in an intermediary variable.

The in parameters work the way that C/C++ programmers are already used to. If you come from Visual Basic, please note that no implicit ByVal or ByRef is done by the compiler—if there is no modifier, the parameters are always passed by value.

This is the point at which I have to seemingly contradict my previous statement: For certain variable types, *by value* actually means *by reference*. Confusing? Not with a bit of background information: Everything in COM is an interface, and every class can have one or more interfaces. An interface is nothing more than an array of function pointers; it does not contain data. Duplicating this array would be a waste of memory resources; therefore, only the start address is copied to the method, which still points to the same address of the interface as the caller. That's why objects pass a reference by value.

ref Parameters

Although you can create many methods using in parameters and return values, you are out of luck as soon as you want to pass a value and have it modified in place (the same memory location, that is). That is where the reference parameter comes in handy:

```
void myMethod(ref int nInOut)
```

Because you pass a variable to the method (and not its value only), the variable nInOut must be initialized. Otherwise, the compiler will complain. Listing 5.2 shows how to create a method with a ref parameter.

Listing 5.2   Passing Parameters by Reference

```
 1: // class SquareSample
 2: using System;
 3:
 4: public class SquareSample
 5: {
 6:    public void CalcSquare(ref int nOne4All)
 7:    {
 8:       nOne4All *= nOne4All;
 9:    }
10: }
11:
12: class SquareApp
13: {
14:    public static void Main()
15:    {
16:       SquareSample sq = new SquareSample();
17:
18:       int nSquaredRef = 20;  // must be initialized
19:       sq.CalcSquare(ref nSquaredRef);
20:       Console.WriteLine(nSquaredRef.ToString());
21:    }
22: }
```

As you can see, all you have to do is to add the ref modifier to both the definition and the call. Because the variable is passed by reference, you can use it to compute the result and pass back the result. However, in a real-world application, I strongly recommend having two variables, one in parameter and one ref parameter.

out Parameters

The third option for passing a parameter is to designate it as an out parameter. As the name implies, an out parameter can be used only to pass a result back from a method. Another difference from the ref parameter is that the caller doesn't need to initialize the variable prior to calling the method. This is shown in Listing 5.3.

Listing 5.3   Defining an out *Parameter*

```
 1: using System;
 2:
 3: public class SquareSample
 4: {
 5:   public void CalcSquare(int nSideLength, out int nSquared)
 6:   {
 7:     nSquared = nSideLength * nSideLength;
 8:   }
 9: }
10:
11: class SquareApp
12: {
13:   public static void Main()
14:   {
15:     SquareSample sq = new SquareSample();
16:
17:     int nSquared;  // need not be initialized
18:     sq.CalcSquare(15, out nSquared);
19:     Console.WriteLine(nSquared.ToString());
20:   }
21: }
```

Overriding Methods

An important principle of object-oriented design is polymorphism. Leaving out theory, *polymorphism* means that in a derived class you can redefine (override) methods of a base class when the programmer of the base class has designed that method for overriding. He can do that using the virtual keyword:

```
virtual void CanBOverridden()
```

All you have to do when deriving from the base class is to add the override keyword to your new method:

```
override void CanBOverridden()
```

When overriding a method of a base class, you must be aware that you cannot change the accessibility of the method—you learn more about access modifiers in a later section of this chapter.

Besides the fact that you can redefine a method of the base class, there is another even more important feature to overriding. When casting the derived class to the base class type and then calling the virtual method, your derived class's method is called, and not the one from the base class.

```
((BaseClass)DerivedClassInstance).CanBOverridden();
```

To demonstrate the concept of virtual methods, Listing 5.4 shows how to create a Triangle base class, which has one member method (ComputeArea) that can be overridden.

Listing 5.4   Overriding a Method of a Base Class

```
 1: using System;
 2:
 3: class Triangle
 4: {
 5:   public virtual double ComputeArea(int a, int b, int c)
 6:   {
 7:     // Heronian formula
 8:     double s = (a + b + c) / 2.0;
 9:     double dArea = Math.Sqrt(s*(s-a)*(s-b)*(s-c));
10:     return dArea;
11:   }
12: }
13:
14: class RightAngledTriangle:Triangle
15: {
16:   public override double ComputeArea(int a, int b, int c)
17:   {
18:     double dArea = a*b/2.0;
19:     return dArea;
20:   }
21: }
22:
23: class TriangleTestApp
```

```
24: {
25:   public static void Main()
26:   {
27:     Triangle tri = new Triangle();
28:     Console.WriteLine(tri.ComputeArea(2, 5, 6));
29:
30:     RightAngledTriangle rat = new RightAngledTriangle();
31:     Console.WriteLine(rat.ComputeArea(3, 4, 5));
32:   }
33: }
```

The base class `Triangle` defines the method `ComputeArea`. It takes three integer parameters, returns a `double` result, and is publicly accessible. Derived from the class `Triangle` is `RightAngledTriangle`, which overrides the `ComputeArea` method and implements its own area calculation formula. Both classes are instantiated and tested in the `Main()` method of the test application class named `TriangleTestApp`.

I owe you an explanation for line 14:

```
class RightAngledTriangle : Triangle
```

The colon (`:`) in the class statement denotes that `RightAngledTriangle` derives from the class `Triangle`. That is all you have to do to let C# know that you want `Triangle` as the base class for `RightAngledTriangle`.

When you take a close look at the `ComputeArea` method for a right-angle triangle, you will see that the third parameter isn't used for the calculation. However, one can create a "right angleness" check by using the third parameter as shown in Listing 5.5.

Listing 5.5   Calling the Base Class Implementation

```
1: class RightAngledTriangle:Triangle
2: {
3:   public override double ComputeArea(int a, int b, int c)
4:   {
5:     const double dEpsilon = 0.0001;
6:     double dArea = 0;
7:     if (Math.Abs((a*a + b*b - c*c)) > dEpsilon)
8:     {
```

continues

Listing 5.5   continued

```
 9:        dArea = base.ComputeArea(a,b,c);
10:     }
11:     else
12:     {
13:        dArea = a*b/2.0;
14:     }
15:
16:     return dArea;
17:   }
18: }
```

The check is simply the formula of Pythagoras, which must yield zero for a right-angled triangle. If the result differs from zero (and a delta epsilon), the class calls the ComputeArea implementation of its base class:

```
dArea = base.ComputeArea(a,b,c);
```

The point of the example is that you can easily call the base class implementation of an overridden method explicitly using the base. qualifier. This is very helpful when you need the functionality implemented in the base class, but don't want to duplicate it in the overridden method.

Method Hiding

A different way of redefining methods is to hide base class methods. This feature is especially valuable when you derive from a class provided by someone else. Look at Listing 5.6, and assume that BaseClass was written by someone else and that you derived DerivedClass from it.

Listing 5.6   Derived Class Implements a Method Not Contained in the Base Class

```
1: using System;
2:
3: class BaseClass
4: {
5: }
6:
7: class DerivedClass:BaseClass
8: {
9:   public void TestMethod()
10:    {
```

```
11:    Console.WriteLine("DerivedClass::TestMethod");
12:    }
13: }
14:
15: class TestApp
16: {
17:    public static void Main()
18:    {
19:      DerivedClass test = new DerivedClass();
20:      test.TestMethod();
21:    }
22: }
```

In this example, your `DerivedClass` implements an additional feature via `TestMethod()`. However, what happens if the developer of the base class thinks that `TestMethod()` is a good idea to have in the base class, and implements it with the same signature? (See Listing 5.7.)

Listing 5.7   Base Class Implements the Same Method as Derived Class

```
1: class BaseClass
2: {
3:   public void TestMethod()
4:   {
5:      Console.WriteLine("BaseClass::TestMethod");
6:   }
7: }
8:
9: class DerivedClass:BaseClass
10: {
11:   public void TestMethod()
12:   {
13:      Console.WriteLine("DerivedClass::TestMethod");
14:   }
15: }
```

In a classic programming language, you would now have a really big problem. C#, however, offers you some advice:

```
hiding2.cs(13,14): warning CS0114: 'DerivedClass.TestMethod()' hides
inherited member 'BaseClass.TestMethod()'. To make the current
method override that implementation, add the override keyword.
Otherwise add the new keyword.
```

With the modifier new, you can tell the compiler that your method should hide the newly added base class method, without you having to rewrite your derived class or code using your derived class. Listing 5.8 shows how to use the new modifier in the example.

Listing 5.8   Hiding the Method of the Base Class

```
 1: class BaseClass
 2: {
 3:   public void TestMethod()
 4:   {
 5:     Console.WriteLine("BaseClass::TestMethod");
 6:   }
 7: }
 8:
 9: class DerivedClass:BaseClass
10: {
11:   new public void TestMethod()
12:   {
13:     Console.WriteLine("DerivedClass::TestMethod");
14:   }
15: }
```

With the addition of the new modifier, the compiler knows that you redefine the base class's method, and that it should hide the base class method. However, if you do the following

```
DerivedClass test = new DerivedClass();
((BaseClass)test).TestMethod();
```

the base class's implementation of TestMethod() is invoked. This behavior is different from overriding the method, where one is guaranteed that the most-derived method is called.

Class Properties

There are two ways to expose named attributes for a class—either via fields or via properties. The former are implemented as member variables with public access; the latter do not correspond directly to a storage location, but are accessed via *accessors*.

The accessors specify the statements that are executed when you want to read or write the value of a property. The accessor for reading a property's value is marked by the keyword get, and the accessor for modifying a value is marked by set.

Before you become cross-eyed from the theory, take a look at the example in Listing 5.9. The property SquareFeet is implemented with get and set accessors.

Listing 5.9 Implementing Property Accessors

```
 1: using System;
 2:
 3: public class House
 4: {
 5:   private int m_nSqFeet;
 6:
 7:   public int SquareFeet
 8:   {
 9:     get { return m_nSqFeet; }
10:     set { m_nSqFeet = value; }
11:   }
12: }
13:
14: class TestApp
15: {
16:   public static void Main()
17:   {
18:     House myHouse = new House();
19:     myHouse.SquareFeet = 250;
20:     Console.WriteLine(myHouse.SquareFeet);
21:   }
22: }
```

The class House has one property named SquareFeet, which can be read and written. The actual value is stored in a variable that is accessible from inside the class—if you want to rewrite it as a field, all you would have to do is leave out the accessors and redefine the variable as

```
public int SquareFeet;
```

For a variable that is simple such as this one, it would be okay. However, if you want to hide details about the inner storage structure of your class, you should resort to accessors. In this case, the set accessor is passed the new value for the property in the `value` parameter. (You can't rename that; see line 10.)

Besides being able to hide implementation details, you are also free to define which operations are allowed:

- `get` and `set` implemented: Read and write access to the property are allowed.

- `get` only: Reading the property value is allowed.

- `set` only: Setting the property's value is the only possible operation.

In addition, you gain the chance to implement validation code in the `set` accessor. For example, you are able to reject a new value for any reason (or none at all). And best of all, no one tells you that it can't be a dynamic property—one that comes into existence only when you request it for the first time, thus delaying resource allocation as long as possible.

Indexers

Did you ever want to include easy indexed access to your class, just like an array? The wait is over with the indexer feature of C#.

Basically, the syntax looks like this:

```
attributes modifiers declarator { declarations }
```

A sample implementation could be

```
public string this[int nIndex]
{
  get { ... }
  set { ... }
}
```

This indexer returns or sets a string at a given index. It has no attributes, but uses the `public` modifier. The *declarator* part consists of type `string` and `this` to denote the class's indexer.

The implementation rules for get and set are the same as for properties. (You can drop either one.) There is one difference, though: You are almost free in defining the parameter list in the square brackets. The restrictions are that you must specify at least one parameter, and ref and out modifiers are not allowed.

The this keyword warrants an explanation. Indexers do not have user-defined names, and this denotes the indexer on the default interface. If your class implements multiple interfaces, you can add more indexers denoted with *InterfaceName*.this.

To demonstrate the use of an indexer, I created a small class that is capable of resolving a hostname to an IP address—or, as is the case for www.microsoft.com, resolving to a list of IP addresses. This list is accessible via an indexer, and you can take a look at the implementation in Listing 5.10.

Listing 5.10   Retrieving IP Addresses by Using an Indexer

```
 1: using System;
 2: using System.Net;
 3:
 4: class ResolveDNS
 5: {
 6:   IPAddress[] m_arrIPs;
 7:
 8:   public void Resolve(string strHost)
 9:   {
10:     IPHostEntry iphe = DNS.GetHostByName(strHost);
11:     m_arrIPs = iphe.AddressList;
12:   }
13:
14:   public IPAddress this[int nIndex]
15:   {
16:     get
17:     {
18:       return m_arrIPs[nIndex];
19:     }
20:   }
21:
22:   public int Count
```

continues

Listing 5.10   continued

```
23:  {
24:     get { return m_arrIPs.Length; }
25:  }
26: }
27:
28: class DNSResolverApp
29: {
30:    public static void Main()
31:    {
32:       ResolveDNS myDNSResolver = new ResolveDNS();
33:       myDNSResolver.Resolve("www.microsoft.com");
34:
35:       int nCount = myDNSResolver.Count;
36:       Console.WriteLine("Found {0} IP's for hostname", nCount);
37:       for (int i=0; i < nCount; i++)
38:          Console.WriteLine(myDNSResolver[i]);
39:    }
40: }
```

To resolve the hostname, I use the DNS class that is part of the
System.Net namespace. However, because this namespace is not
contained in the core library, I had to reference the library in my
compiler statement:

```
csc /r:System.Net.dll /out:resolver.exe dnsresolve.cs
```

The resolver code is straightforward. In the Resolve method, the code
calls the static GetHostByName method of the DNS class, which returns an
IPHostEntry object. This object, in turn, contains the array I am looking
for—the AddressList array. Before exiting the Resolve method, I store a
copy the AddressList array (objects of type IPAddress are stored inside
it) locally in the object's instance member m_arrIPs.

With the array now populated, the application code can enumerate the IP
addresses in lines 37 and 38 by using the indexer implemented in the
class ResolveDNS. (There is more information about for statements in
Chapter 6, "Control Statements.") Because there is no way to modify the
IP addresses, only get is implemented for the indexer. For simplicity's
sake, I leave out-of-bounds checking to the array.

Events

When you write a class, you sometimes have a need to let clients of your class know that a certain event has occurred. If you are a longtime programmer, you have seen many different ways of achieving this, including function pointers for callback and event sinks for ActiveX controls. Now you are going to learn another way of attaching client code to class notifications—with events.

Events can be declared either as class fields (member variables) or as properties. Both approaches share the commonality that the event's type must be `delegate`, which is C#'s equivalent to a function pointer prototype.

Each event can be consumed by zero or more clients, and a client can attach and detach from the event at any time. You can implement the delegates as either static or instance methods, with the latter being a welcome feature for C++ programmers.

Now that I have mentioned all the main features of events as well as the corresponding delegates, please take a look at the example in Listing 5.11. It presents the theory in action.

Listing 5.11   Implementing an Event Handler in Your Class

```
1: using System;
2:
3: // forward declaration
4: public delegate void EventHandler(string strText);
5:
6: class EventSource
7: {
8:    public event EventHandler TextOut;
9:
10:    public void TriggerEvent()
11:    {
12:      if (null != TextOut) TextOut("Event triggered");
13:    }
14: }
15:
```

continues

Listing 5.11   continued

```
16: class TestApp
17: {
18:    public static void Main()
19:    {
20:      EventSource evsrc = new EventSource();
21:
22:      evsrc.TextOut += new EventHandler(CatchEvent);
23:      evsrc.TriggerEvent();
24:
25:      evsrc.TextOut -= new EventHandler(CatchEvent);
26:      evsrc.TriggerEvent();
27:
28:      TestApp theApp = new TestApp();
29:      evsrc.TextOut += new EventHandler(theApp.InstanceCatch);
30:      evsrc.TriggerEvent();
31:    }
32:
33:    public static void CatchEvent(string strText)
34:    {
35:      Console.WriteLine(strText);
36:    }
37:
38:    public void InstanceCatch(string strText)
39:    {
40:      Console.WriteLine("Instance " + strText);
41:    }
42: }
```

Line 4 declares the delegate (the event method prototype), which is used to declare the TextOut event field for the EventSource class in line 8. You can view the delegate declaration as a new kind of type that can be used when declaring events.

The class has only one method, which allows us to trigger the event. Note that you have to check the event field against null because it could happen that no one is interested in the event.

The class TestApp houses the Main method, as well as two methods with the necessary signature for the event. One of the methods is static, and the other is an instance method.

The EventSource class is instantiated, and the static method is subscribed to the TextOut event:

```
evsrc.TextOut += new EventHandler(CatchEvent);
```

From now on, this method is called when the event is triggered. If you are no longer interested in the event, simply unsubscribe:

```
evsrc.TextOut -= new EventHandler(CatchEvent);
```

Note that you cannot unsubscribe handlers at will—only those that were created in your class's code. To prove that event handlers work with instance methods, too, the remaining code creates an instance of TestApp and hooks up the event handler method.

Where will events be most useful for you? You will often deal with events and delegates in ASP+ as well as when using the WFC (Windows Foundation Classes).

Applying Modifiers

During the course of this chapter, you have already seen modifiers such as public, virtual, and so on. To summarize them in an easily accessible manner, I have split them into the following three sections:

- Class modifiers
- Member modifiers
- Access modifiers

Class Modifiers

So far, I haven't dealt with class modifiers other than the access modifiers applied to classes. However, there are two modifiers you can use for classes:

- abstract—The most important point about an abstract class is that it cannot be instantiated. Only derived classes that are not abstract can be instantiated. The derived class must implement all abstract members of the abstract base class. You cannot apply the sealed modifier to an abstract class.

• sealed—Sealed classes cannot be inherited. Use this modifier to prevent accidental inheritance; some classes in the NGWS framework use this modifier.

To see both modifiers in action, look at Listing 5.12, which creates a sealed class based on an abstract one (definitely a quite extreme example).

Listing 5.12   Abstract and Sealed Classes

```
 1: using System;
 2:
 3: abstract class AbstractClass
 4: {
 5:   abstract public void MyMethod();
 6: }
 7:
 8: sealed class DerivedClass:AbstractClass
 9: {
10:   public override void MyMethod()
11:   {
12:     Console.WriteLine("sealed class");
13:   }
14: }
15:
16: public class TestApp
17: {
18:   public static void Main()
19:   {
20:     DerivedClass dc = new DerivedClass();
21:     dc.MyMethod();
22:   }
23: }
```

Member Modifiers

The number of class modifiers is small compared to the number of member modifiers that are available. I have already presented some of these, and forthcoming examples in this book describe the other member modifiers.

The following member modifiers are available:

- abstract—Indicates that a method or accessor does not contain an implementation. Both are implicitly virtual, and in the inheriting class, you must provide the override keyword.

- const—This modifier applies to fields and local variables. The constant expression is evaluated at compile time; therefore, it cannot contain references to variables.

- event—Defines a field or property as type event. Used to bind client code to events of the class.

- extern—Tells the compiler that the method is actually implemented externally. Chapter 10, "Interoperating with Unmanaged Code," deals with external code extensively.

- override—Used to modify a method or accessor that is defined virtual in any of the base classes. The signature of the overriding and base method must be the same.

- readonly—A field declared with the readonly modifier can be changed only in its declaration or in the constructor of the containing class.

- static—Members that are declared static belong to the class, and not to an instance of the class. You can use static with fields, methods, properties, operators, and even constructors.

- virtual—Indicates that the method or accessor can be overridden by inheriting classes.

Access Modifiers

Access modifiers define the level of access that certain code has to class members, such as methods and properties. You have to apply the desired access modifier to each member; otherwise, the default access type is implied.

You can apply one of the following four access modifiers:

- `public`—The member is accessible from anywhere; this is the least restrictive access modifier.

- `protected`—The member is accessible in the class and all derived classes. No access from outside is permitted.

- `private`—Only code inside the same class can access this member. Even derived classes cannot access it.

- `internal`—Access is granted to all code that is part of the same NGWS component (application or library). You can view it as public at the NGWS component level, private for the outside.

To illustrate the use of access modifiers, I have modified the `Triangle` example just a bit to contain additional fields and a new derived class (see Listing 5.13).

Listing 5.13   Using Access Modifiers in Your Classes

```
 1: using System;
 2:
 3: internal class Triangle
 4: {
 5:    protected int m_a, m_b, m_c;
 6:    public Triangle(int a, int b, int c)
 7:    {
 8:      m_a = a;
 9:      m_b = b;
10:      m_c = c;
11:    }
12:
13:    public virtual double Area()
14:    {
15:      // Heronian formula
16:      double s = (m_a + m_b + m_c) / 2.0;
17:      double dArea = Math.Sqrt(s*(s-m_a)*(s-m_b)*(s-m_c));
18:      return dArea;
19:    }
20: }
21:
22: internal class Prism:Triangle
23: {
```

```
24:    private int m_h;
25:    public Prism(int a, int b, int c, int h):base(a,b,c)
26:    {
27:      m_h = h;
28:    }
29:
30:    public override double Area()
31:    {
32:      double dArea = base.Area() * 2.0;
33:      dArea += m_a*m_h + m_b*m_h + m_c*m_h;
34:      return dArea;
35:    }
36: }
37:
38: class PrismApp
39: {
40:   public static void Main()
41:   {
42:     Prism prism = new Prism(2,5,6,1);
43:     Console.WriteLine(prism.Area());
44:   }
45: }
```

Both the `Triangle` and the `Prism` class are now marked as `internal`. This means that they are accessible only in the current NGWS component. Please remember that the term NGWS component refers to packaging, and not to the *component* that you may be used to from COM+. The `Triangle` class has three protected members, which are initialized in the constructor and used in the `Area` calculation method. Because these members are protected, I can access them in the derived class `Prism` to perform a different `Area` calculation there. `Prism` itself adds an additional member m_h, which is `private`—not even a derived class could access it.

It is generally a good idea to invest time in planning the kind of protection level you want for each class member, and even for each class. Thorough planning helps you later when changes need to be introduced because no programmer could have possibly used "undocumented" functionality of your class.

Summary

This chapter showed the various elements of a class, which is the template for the running instances, the objects. The first code that is executed in the lifetime of an object is the constructor. The constructor is used to initialize variables, which can be later used in methods to compute results.

Methods enable you to pass values, pass references to variables, or transport an output value only. Methods can be overridden to implement new functionality, or you can hide base class members that implement a method with the same signature.

Named attributes can be implemented either as fields (member variables) or property accessors. The latter are get and set accessors, and by leaving out one or the other, you can create write-only or read-only properties. Accessors are well suited for validation of value assignment to properties.

Another feature of a C# class is indexers, which make it possible to access values in a class with an array-like syntax. And, if you want clients to be notified when something happens in your class, you can have them subscribe to events.

The life of an object ends when the garbage collector invokes the destructor. Because you cannot determine exactly when this will happen, you should create a method to release expensive resources as soon as you are done using them.

CHAPTER 6

Control Statements

- Selection Statements
- Iteration Statements

There is one kind of statement that you will find in every programming language—control of flow statements. In this chapter, I present C#'s control statements, split into two major sections:

- Selection statements
- Iteration statements

If you are a C or C++ programmer, most of this information will look very familiar to you; however, there are some differences you must be aware of.

Selection Statements

When employing selection statements, you define a controlling statement whose value controls which statement is executed. Two selection statements are available in C#:

- The `if` statement
- The `switch` statement

The *if* Statement

The first and most commonly used selection statement is the `if` statement. Whether the embedded statement is executed is determined by a Boolean expression:

```
if (boolean-expression) embedded-statement
```

Of course, you also can have an `else` branch that is executed when the Boolean expression evaluates to false:

```
if (boolean-expression) embedded-statement else  embedded-statement
```

An example is to check for a nonzero-length string before executing certain statements:

```
if (0 != strTest.Length)
{
}
```

This is a Boolean expression. (`!=` means not equal.) However, if you come from C or C++, you might be used to writing code like this:

```
if (strTest.Length)
{
}
```

This no longer works in C# because the `if` statement only allows for results of the `bool` data type, and the `Length` property of the string object returns an integer. The compiler will complain with this error message:

```
error CS0029: Cannot implicitly convert type 'int' to 'bool'
```

The downside is that you have to change your habits; however, the upside is that you will never again be bitten with assignment errors in `if` clauses:

```
if (nMyValue = 5) ...
```

The correct code would be

```
if (nMyValue == 5) ...
```

because comparison for equality is performed with ==, just as in C and C++. Look at the following available comparison operators (not all are valid for every data type, though!):

- ==—Returns true if both values are the same.
- !=—Returns true if the values are different.
- <, <=, >, >=—Returns true if the values fulfill the relation (less than, less than or equal, greater, greater than or equal).

Each of these operators is implemented via operator overloading, and the implementation is specific to the data type. If you compare two variables of different type, an implicit conversion must exist for the compiler to create the necessary code automatically. You can, however, perform an explicit cast.

The code in Listing 6.1 demonstrates a few different usage scenarios of the `if` statement, as well as how to use the `string` data type. The basic idea behind this program is to determine whether the first argument passed to the application starts with an uppercase letter, lowercase letter, or digit.

Listing 6.1   Determining the Case of a Letter

```
1: using System;
2:
3: class NestedIfApp
4: {
5:   public static int Main(string[] args)
6:   {
```

continues

Listing 6.1   continued

```
 7:     if (args.Length != 1)
 8:     {
 9:       Console.WriteLine("Usage: one argument");
10:       return 1;  // error level
11:     }
12:
13:     char chLetter = args[0][0];
14:
15:     if (chLetter >= 'A')
16:       if (chLetter <= 'Z')
17:       {
18:         Console.WriteLine("{0} is uppercase",chLetter);
19:         return 0;
20:       }
21:
22:     chLetter = Char.FromString(args[0]);
23:     if (chLetter >= 'a' && chLetter <= 'z')
24:       Console.WriteLine("{0} is lowercase",chLetter);
25:
26:     if (Char.IsDigit((chLetter = args[0][0])))
27:       Console.WriteLine("{0} is a digit",chLetter);
28:
29:     return 0;
30:   }
31: }
```

The first if block starting in line 7 checks for the existence of exactly one string in the args array. If the condition is not met, the program writes a usage message to the console and terminates.

Extracting a single character from a string can be done in multiple ways—either by using the char indexer as shown in line 13 or by using the static FromString method of the Char class, which returns the first character of a string.

The if block in lines 16–20 checks for an uppercase letter by using a nested if block. Checking for a lowercase letter is done using the logical AND operator (&&), and the final check for digits is performed using the IsDigit static function of the Char class.

Besides the && operator, there is a second conditional logical operator, which is || for OR. Both conditional logical operators are short-circuited. For the && operator, that means the first non-true result of a conditional AND expression returns false, and the remaining conditional AND expressions are not evaluated. The || operator, in contrast, is short-circuited when the first true conditional is met.

What I want to get across is that, to cut computing time, you should put the expression that is most likely to short-circuit the evaluation at the front. Also, you should be aware that computing certain values in an if statement is potentially dangerous:

```
if (1 == 1 || (5 == (strLength=str.Length)))
{
  Console.WriteLine(strLength);
}
```

This is, of course, a greatly exaggerated example, but it shows the point—the first statement evaluates to true, and hence the second statement is not executed, which leaves the variable strLength at its original value. It is good advice to never put assignments in if statements that have conditional logical operators!

The *switch* Statement

In contrast to the if statement, the switch statement has one controlling expression and embedded statements are executed based on the constant value of the controlling expression they are associated with. The general syntax of the switch statement looks like this:

```
switch (controlling-expression)
{
  case constant-expression:
    embedded-statements
  default:
    embedded-statements
}
```

The allowed data types for the controlling expression are sbyte, byte, short, ushort, uint, long, ulong, char, string, or an enumeration type.

As long as an implicit conversion to any of these types exists for a different data type, it is fine to use it as controlling expression, too.

The switch statement is executed in the following order:

1. The controlling expression is evaluated.

2. If a constant expression in a case label matches the value of the evaluated controlling expression, the embedded statements are executed.

3. If no constant expression matches the controlling expression, the embedded statements in the default label are executed.

4. If there is no match for a case label, and there is no default label, control is transferred to the end of the switch block.

Before moving on to more details of the switch statement, take a look at Listing 6.2, which shows a switch statement in action for displaying the number of days in a month (ignoring leap years).

Listing 6.2   Using a switch *Statement to Display the Days in a Month*

```
1: using System;
2:
3: class FallThrough
4: {
5:   public static void Main(string[] args)
6:   {
7:     if (args.Length != 1) return;
8:
9:     int nMonth = Int32.Parse(args[0]);
10:    if (nMonth < 1 || nMonth > 12) return;
11:    int nDays = 0;
12:
13:    switch (nMonth)
14:    {
15:      case 2: nDays = 28; break;
16:      case 4:
17:      case 6:
18:      case 9:
19:      case 11: nDays = 30; break;
20:      default: nDays = 31;
21:    }
```

```
22:    Console.WriteLine("{0} days in this month",nDays);
23:   }
24: }
```

The switch block is contained in lines 13–21. For a C programmer, this looks very familiar because it doesn't use break statements. However, there is one important difference that makes life easier: You must add the break statement (or a different jump statement) because the compiler will complain that fall-through to the next section is not allowed in C#.

What is *fall-through*? In C (and C++), it was perfectly legal to leave out break and write the following code:

```
nVar = 1
switch (nVar)
{
  case 1:
    DoSomething();
  case 2:
    DoMore();
}
```

In this example, after executing the code for the first case statement, execution would fall-through and execute code in other case labels until a break statement exits the switch block. Although this is sometimes a powerful feature, more often it was the cause of hard-to-find bugs. That is why you don't find fall-through in C#.

But what if you want to execute code in other case labels? There is a way, and it is shown in Listing 6.3.

Listing 6.3 *Using* goto label *and* goto default *in a* switch *Statement*

```
1: using System;
2:
3: class SwitchApp
4: {
5:   public static void Main()
6:   {
7:     Random objRandom = new Random();
8:     double dRndNumber = objRandom.NextDouble();
9:     int nRndNumber = (int)(dRndNumber * 10.0);
10:
```

continues

Listing 6.3   continued

```
11:     switch (nRndNumber)
12:     {
13:       case 1:
14:           // do nothing
15:           break;
16:       case 2:
17:           goto case 3;
18:       case 3:
19:           Console.WriteLine("Handler for 2 and 3");
20:           break;
21:       case 4:
22:           goto default;
23:           // everything beyond a goto will be warned as
24:           // unreachable code
25:       default:
26:           Console.WriteLine("Random number {0}", nRndNumber);
27:     }
28:   }
29: }
```

In this example, I generate the value to be used as the controlling expression via the Random class (lines 7–9). The switch block contains two jump statements that are valid for the switch statement:

- goto case *label*: Jump to the label indicated
- goto default: Jump to the default label

With these two jump statements, you can create the same functionality as in C, however, the fall-through is no longer automatic. You have to explicitly request it.

A further implication of the fall-through feature no longer being available is that you can arbitrarily arrange the labels, such a putting the default label in front of all other labels. To illustrate it, I created an example with an intentional endless loop:

```
switch (nSomething)
{
default:
case 5:
   goto default;
}
```

I have saved the discussion of one of the `switch` statement's features until the end—the fact that you can use strings as constant expressions. This might not sound like big news for Visual Basic programmers, but it is a new feature that programmers coming from C or C++ will like.

Now, a `switch` statement can check for string constants as shown here

```
string strTest = "Chris";
switch (strTest)
{
  case "Chris":
    Console.WriteLine("Hello Chris!");
    break;
}
```

Iteration Statements

When you want to execute a certain statement or block of statements repeatedly, C# offers you a choice of four different iteration statements to use depending on the task at hand:

- The `for` statement

- The `foreach` statement

- The `while` statement

- The `do` statement

The *for* Statement

The `for` statement is especially useful when you know up front how many times an embedded statement should be executed. However, the general syntax permits you to repeatedly execute an embedded statement (as well as the iteration expression) while a condition is true:

```
for (initializer; condition; iterator) embedded-statement
```

Please note that *initializer*, `condition`, and *iterator* are all optional. If you leave out the `condition`, you can create an endless loop that can be exited with a jump statement (`break` or `goto`) only, as shown in the following code snippet:

```
for (;;)
{
  break;  // for some reason
}
```

Another important point is that you can add multiple statements, separated by commas, to all the three arguments of the for loop. For example, you could initialize two variables, have three conditional statements, and iterate four variables.

As a C or C++ programmer, there is only one change you must be aware of: The condition must evaluate to a Boolean expression, just as in the if statement.

Listing 6.4 contains an example of using the for statement. It shows how to compute a factorial a bit faster than with recursive function calls.

Listing 6.4 Computing a Factorial in a for *Loop*

```
 1: using System;
 2:
 3: class Factorial
 4: {
 5:   public static void Main(string[] args)
 6:   {
 7:     long nFactorial = 1;
 8:     long nComputeTo = Int64.Parse(args[0]);
 9:
10:     long nCurDig = 1;
11:     for (nCurDig=1;nCurDig <= nComputeTo; nCurDig++)
12:       nFactorial *= nCurDig;
13:
14:     Console.WriteLine("{0}! is {1}",nComputeTo, nFactorial);
15:   }
16: }
```

The example is overly lengthy, but it serves as a starting point to show what one can do with for statements. First, I could have declared the variable nCurDig inside the initializer part:

```
for (long nCurDig=1;nCurDig <= nComputeTo; nCurDig++) nFactorial *=
➥nCurDig;
```

Another option would have been to leave out the initializer as in the following line, because line 10 initializes the variable outside the `for` statement. (Remember: C# requires initialized variables!):

```
for (;nCurDig <= nComputeTo; nCurDig++) nFactorial *= nCurDig;
```

Another change might be to move the ++ operation to the summation embedded statement:

```
for ( ;nCurDig <= nComputeTo; ) nFactorial *= nCurDig++;
```

If I also want to get rid of the conditional statement, all I have to do is add an `if` statement to terminate the loop using a `break` statement:

```
for (;;)
{
  if (nCurDig > nComputeTo) break;
  nFactorial *= nCurDig++;
}
```

Besides the `break` statement, which is used to exit the `for` statement, you can use `continue` to skip the current iteration and continue with the next.

```
for (;nCurDig <= nComputeTo;)
{
  if (5 == nCurDig) continue; // this "jumps" over remaining code
  nFactorial *= nCurDig++;
}
```

The *foreach* Statement

A feature that has been present in Visual Basic languages for a long time is that of collection enumeration by using the `For Each` statement. C# also has a command for enumerating elements of a collection via the `foreach` statement:

```
foreach (Type identifier in expression) embedded-statement
```

The iteration variable is declared by type and identifier, and expression corresponds to the collection. The iteration variable represents the collection element for which an iteration is currently performed.

You have to be aware that you cannot assign a new value to the iteration variable, nor can you pass it to a function as a `ref` or `out` parameter. This refers to code that is executed in the embedded statement.

How can you tell whether a certain class supports the `foreach` statement? The short version is that the class must support a method with the signature `GetEnumerator()`, and the struct, class, or interface returned by it must have the public method `MoveNext()` and the public property `Current`. If you want to know more, please look at the language reference, which has a lot of detail on this topic.

For the example in Listing 6.5, I happened to pick a class that, by chance, implements all these requirements. I use it to enumerate all environment variables that are defined.

Listing 6.5   Reading All Environment Variables

```
 1: using System;
 2: using System.Collections;
 3:
 4: class EnvironmentDumpApp
 5: {
 6:   public static void Main()
 7:   {
 8:     IDictionary envvars = Environment.GetEnvironmentVariables();
 9:     Console.WriteLine("There are {0} environment variables
        ➥declared", envvars.Keys.Count);
10:     foreach (String strKey in envvars.Keys)
11:     {
12:       Console.WriteLine("{0} = {1}",strKey,
          ➥envvars[strKey].ToString());
13:     }
14:   }
15: }
```

The call to `GetEnvironmentVariables` (line 8) returns an interface of type `IDictionary`, which is the dictionary interface implemented by many classes in the NGWS framework. Two collections are accessible through the `IDictionary` interface: `Keys` and `Values`. In this example, I use `Keys` in the `foreach` statement, and then do a lookup for the value based on the current key value (line 12).

There is one single caution when using `foreach`: You should take extra care when deciding about the type of the iteration variable. Choosing a wrong type isn't necessarily detected by the compiler, but it is detected at runtime and it causes an exception.

The *while* Statement

When you want to execute an embedded statement zero or more times, the `while` statement is what you are looking for:

```
while (conditional) embedded-statement
```

The conditional statement—it is once again a Boolean expression—controls how often (if at all) the embedded statement is executed. You can use the `break` and `continue` statements to control execution in the `while` statement, which behave exactly the same way as in the `for` statement.

To illustrate the usage of `while`, Listing 6.6 shows you how to use the `StreamReader` class to output a C# source file to the console.

Listing 6.6   Displaying a File's Content

```
 1: using System;
 2: using System.IO;
 3:
 4: class WhileDemoApp
 5: {
 6:   public static void Main()
 7:   {
 8:     StreamReader sr = File.OpenText ("whilesample.cs");
 9:     String strLine = null;
10:
11:     while (null != (strLine = sr.ReadLine()))
12:     {
13:         Console.WriteLine(strLine);
14:     }
15:
16:     sr.Close();
17:   }
18: }
```

The code opens the file `whilesample.cs`, and while the method `ReadLine` returns a string different from `null`, outputs the read string to the console. Note that I use an assignment in the while conditional. If there were more conditions linked with either && or | |, I shouldn't rely on the fact that they are executed because of possible short-circuiting.

The *do* Statement

The final iteration statement available with C# is the do statement. It is very similar to the while statement, only the condition is checked after the first iteration:

```
do
{
   embedded statements
}
while (condition);
```

The do statement guarantees at least one execution of the embedded statements, and as long as the condition evaluates to true, they continue to be executed. You can force execution to leave the do block by using the break statement. If you want to skip only one iteration, use the continue statement.

An example of how to use a do statement is presented in Listing 6.7. It requests one or more numbers from the user, and computes the average when execution leaves the do loop.

Listing 6.7   Computing the Average in a do *Loop*

```
 1: using System;
 2:
 3: class ComputeAverageApp
 4: {
 5:   public static void Main()
 6:   {
 7:     ComputeAverageApp theApp = new ComputeAverageApp();
 8:     theApp.Run();
 9:   }
10:
11:   public void Run()
12:   {
13:     double dValue = 0;
14:     double dSum = 0;
15:     int nNoOfValues = 0;
```

```
16:     char chContinue = 'y';
17:     string strInput;
18:
19:     do
20:     {
21:       Console.Write("Enter a value: ");
22:       strInput = Console.ReadLine();
23:       dValue = Double.Parse(strInput);
24:       dSum += dValue;
25:       nNoOfValues++;
26:       Console.Write("Read another value?");
27:
28:       strInput = Console.ReadLine();
29:       chContinue = Char.FromString(strInput);
30:     }
31:     while ('y' == chContinue);
32:
33:     Console.WriteLine("The average is {0}",dSum / nNoOfValues);
34:   }
35: }
```

In this example, I instantiate an object of type ComputeAverageApp in the static Main function. It also then invokes the Run method of the instance, which contains all functionality necessary to compute the average.

The do loop spans lines 19–31. The condition is designed around whether the user decides to add another value by answering y to the respective question. Any other character causes execution to exit the do block, and the average is computed.

As you can see from the example presented, the do statement does not differ much from the while statement—the only difference is when the condition is evaluated.

Summary

This chapter explained how to use the various selection and iteration statements that are available in C#. The if statement is the statement you are likely to use most often in your programs. The compiler will take care for you when it comes to enforcing Boolean expressions. However, you must make sure that the short-circuiting of conditional statements doesn't prevent necessary code from executing.

The `switch` statement—although also similar to its counterpart in the C world—has been improved, too. Fall-throughs are no longer supported, and you can use string labels, which are new for C programmers.

In the last part of this chapter, I showed how to use the `for`, `foreach`, `while`, and `do` statements. The statements fulfill various needs, including executing a fixed number of iterations, enumerating collection elements, and executing statements an arbitrary number of times based on some condition.

CHAPTER 7

Exception Handling

- Checked and Unchecked Statements
- Exception-Handling Statements
- Throwing Exceptions
- Do's and Donts of Exception Handling

One big advantage of the NGWS runtime is that exception handling is standardized across languages. An exception thrown in C# can be handled in a Visual Basic client. No more HRESULTs or ISupportErrorInfo interfaces.

Although that cross-language exception handling is great, this chapter focuses entirely on C# exception handling. First, you slightly change the overflow-handling behavior of the compiler, and then the fun begins: You handle the exceptions. To add a further twist, you later throw exceptions that you created.

Checked and Unchecked Statements

When you perform a calculation, it can happen that the computed result exceeds the valid range of the result variable's data type. This situation is called an *overflow*, and depending on the programming language, you are notified in some way—or not at all. (Does that sound familiar to C++ programmers?)

So, how does C# handle overflows? To find out about its default behavior, look at the factorial example I presented earlier in this book. (For your convenience, the earlier example is given again in Listing 7.1.)

Listing 7.1   Calculating the Factorial of a Number

```
 1: using System;
 2:
 3: class Factorial
 4: {
 5:   public static void Main(string[] args)
 6:   {
 7:     long nFactorial = 1;
 8:     long nComputeTo = Int64.Parse(args[0]);
 9:
10:     long nCurDig = 1;
11:     for (nCurDig=1;nCurDig <= nComputeTo; nCurDig++)
12:       nFactorial *= nCurDig;
13:
14:     Console.WriteLine("{0}! is {1}",nComputeTo, nFactorial);
15:   }
16: }
```

When you execute the program with a command line such as

```
factorial 2000
```

the result presented is 0, and nothing else happens. Therefore, it is safe to assume that C# silently handles overflow situations and does not explicitly warn you.

You can change this behavior by enabling overflow checking either for the entire application (via a compiler switch) or on a statement-by-statement basis. Each of the following two sections tackles one of the solutions.

Compiler Settings for Overflow Checking

If you want to control overflow checking for the entire application, the C#
compiler setting `checked` is what you are looking for. By default, overflow
checking is disabled. To explicitly request it, run the following compiler
command:

```
csc factorial.cs /checked+
```

Now when you execute the application with a parameter of `2000`, the
NGWS runtime notifies you about the overflow exception (see Figure 7.1).

Figure 7.1

With overflow checking enabled, the factorial code generates an exception.

Dismissing the dialog box with the OK button reveals the exception
message:

```
Exception occurred: System.OverflowException
    at Factorial.Main(System.String[])
```

Now you know that overflow conditions throw a
`System.OverflowException`. How to catch and handle such an exception
is presented after we finish programmatic overflow checking in the next
section.

Programmatic Overflow Checking

If you do not want to enable overflow checking for your entire
application, you might be more comfortable by enabling it only for
certain code blocks. For this scenario, you can use `checked` statement as
presented in Listing 7.2.

Listing 7.2 Checking for Overflow in the Factorial Calculation

```
 1: using System;
 2:
 3: class Factorial
 4: {
 5:   public static void Main(string[] args)
 6:   {
 7:     long nFactorial = 1;
 8:     long nComputeTo = Int64.Parse(args[0]);
 9:
10:     long nCurDig = 1;
11:
12:     for (nCurDig=1;nCurDig <= nComputeTo; nCurDig++)
13:       checked { nFactorial *= nCurDig; }
14:
15:     Console.WriteLine("{0}! is {1}",nComputeTo, nFactorial);
16:   }
17: }
```

Even if you compile this code with the flag checked-, overflow checking is still performed for the multiplication in line 13 because a checked statement encloses it. The error message will remain the same.

A statement that exhibits the opposite behavior is unchecked. Even if you enable overflow checking (checked+ flag for the compiler), the code enclosed by the unchecked statement will not raise overflow exceptions:

```
unchecked
{
  nFactorial *= nCurDig;
}
```

Exception-Handling Statements

Now that you know how to generate an exception (and you'll find many more ways, trust me), there is still the question of how to deal with it. If you are a C++ WIN32 programmer, you are definitely familiar with SEH (Structured Exception Handling). You will find it comforting that the commands in C# are almost the same, and that they also behave in a similar way.

The following three sections introduce C#'s exception-handling statements:

- Catching with `try-catch`
- Cleaning up with `try-finally`
- Handling all with `try-catch-finally`

Catching with *try* and *catch*

You are definitely most interested about one thing—not presenting that nasty exception message to the user so that your application continues to execute. For this to happen, you must catch (handle) the exception.

The statements used for this are `try` and `catch`. `try` encloses the statements that might throw an exception, whereas `catch` handles an exception if one exists. Listing 7.3 implements exception handling for the `OverflowException` using `try` and `catch`.

Listing 7.3   *Catching the* `OverflowException` *Raised by the Factorial Calculation*

```
 1: using System;
 2:
 3: class Factorial
 4: {
 5:   public static void Main(string[] args)
 6:   {
 7:     long nFactorial = 1, nCurDig=1;
 8:     long nComputeTo = Int64.Parse(args[0]);
 9:
10:     try
11:     {
12:       checked
13:       {
14:         for (;nCurDig <= nComputeTo; nCurDig++)
15:           nFactorial *= nCurDig;
16:       }
17:     }
18:     catch (OverflowException oe)
```

continues

Listing 7.3   continued

```
19:    {
20:        Console.WriteLine("Computing {0} caused an overflow
           ➥exception", nComputeTo);
21:        return;
22:    }
23:
24:    Console.WriteLine("{0}! is {1}",nComputeTo, nFactorial);
25:  }
26: }
```

For clarity, I have expanded some of the code blocks, and I have also made sure that exceptions are generated using the checked statement even if you forget the compiler setting.

Exception handling is really no big deal, as you can see. All you need to do is to enclose the exception-prone code in a try statement, and then catch the exception, which, in this case, is of type OverflowException. Whenever an exception is thrown, the code in the catch block takes care of proper processing.

If you do not know in advance which kind of exception to expect but still want to be on the safe side, you can simply omit the type of the exception:

```
try
{
...
}
catch
{
...
}
```

However, with this approach, you cannot get access to the exception object, which contains important error information. The generalized exception-handling code then looks like this:

```
try
{
...
}
```

```
catch(System.Exception e)
{
...
}
```

Note that you cannot pass the e object to a method with `ref` or `out` modifiers, nor can you assign it a different value.

Cleaning Up with *try* and *finally*

If you are more concerned about cleanup than error handling, the `try` and `finally` construct will catch your fancy. It does not suppress the error message, but all the code contained in the `finally` block is still executed after the exception is raised.

Although your program terminates abnormally, you can get a message to the user, as shown in Listing 7.4.

Listing 7.4   Handling Exceptional Conditions in the `finally` Statement

```
 1: using System;
 2:
 3: class Factorial
 4: {
 5:   public static void Main(string[] args)
 6:   {
 7:     long nFactorial = 1, nCurDig=1;
 8:     long nComputeTo = Int64.Parse(args[0]);
 9:     bool bAllFine = false;
10:
11:     try
12:     {
13:       checked
14:       {
15:         for (;nCurDig <= nComputeTo; nCurDig++)
16:           nFactorial *= nCurDig;
17:       }
18:       bAllFine = true;
19:     }
20:     finally
21:     {
22:       if (!bAllFine)
```

continues

Listing 7.4   continued

```
23:            Console.WriteLine("Computing {0} caused an overflow
               ➥exception", nComputeTo);
24:        else
25:            Console.WriteLine("{0}! is {1}",nComputeTo,
               ➥nFactorial);
26:    }
27:    }
28: }
```

By examining the code, you might guess that `finally` is executed even when no exception is raised. This is true—the code in `finally` is always executed, with or without an exception condition. To illustrate how to provide some meaningful information to the user in both cases, I introduced the new variable `bAllFine`. `bAllFine` tells the `finally` block whether it was called because of an exception or just because the calculation completed successfully.

As a programmer used to SEH, you might be wondering whether there is an equivalent to the `__leave` statement that is available in C++. If you don't know it already, the `__leave` statement is used in C++ to prematurely stop executing code in the `try` block, and to jump immediately to the `finally` block.

The bad news is, the `__leave` statement isn't in C#. However, the code in Listing 7.5 demonstrates a solution that you can implement.

Listing 7.5   Jumping from the `try` to the `finally` Statement

```
1: using System;
2:
3: class JumpTest
4: {
5:   public static void Main()
6:   {
7:     try
8:     {
9:       Console.WriteLine("try");
10:      goto __leave;
```

```
11:    }
12:    finally
13:    {
14:       Console.WriteLine("finally");
15:    }
16:
17:       __leave:
18:       Console.WriteLine("__leave");
19:    }
20: }
```

When this application is run, the output is

```
try
finally
__leave
```

A goto statement can't exit a finally block. Even placing the goto statement in the try block returns control immediately to the finally block. Therefore, the goto just leaves the try block and jumps to the finally block. The __leave label isn't reached until all code in finally finishes execution. In this way, you can simulate the __leave statement that was present for SEH.

By the way, you might suspect that the goto statement was ignored because it was the last statement in the try block and control was automatically transferred to finally. To prove that is not the case, try placing the goto statement before the Console.WriteLine method call. Although you will get a compiler warning because of unreachable code, you'll see that the goto is actually being executed and no output is being generated for the try string.

Handling All with *try-catch-finally*

The most likely approach for your applications is to merge the prior two error-handling techniques—catch the error, clean up, and continue executing the application. All you need to do is use try, catch, and finally statements in your error-handling code. Listing 7.6 shows the approach for dealing with division-by-zero errors.

Listing 7.6   Implementing Multiple `catch` *Statements*

```
 1: using System;
 2:
 3: class CatchIT
 4: {
 5:   public static void Main()
 6:   {
 7:     try
 8:     {
 9:       int nTheZero = 0;
10:       int nResult = 10 / nTheZero;
11:     }
12:     catch(DivideByZeroException divEx)
13:     {
14:       Console.WriteLine("divide by zero occurred!");
15:     }
16:     catch(Exception Ex)
17:     {
18:       Console.WriteLine("some other exception");
19:     }
20:     finally
21:     {
22:     }
23:   }
24: }
```

The twist with this example is that it contains multiple `catch` statements. The first one catches the more likely `DivideByZeroException` exception, whereas the second `catch` statement deals with all remaining exceptions by catching the general exception.

You must always catch specialized exceptions first, followed by more general exceptions. What happens if you don't catch exceptions in this order is illustrated by the code in Listing 7.7.

Listing 7.7   Inappropriate Ordering of `catch` *Statements*

```
 1:    try
 2:    {
 3:      int nTheZero = 0;
 4:      int nResult = 10 / nTheZero;
 5:    }
```

```
 6:     catch(Exception Ex)
 7:     {
 8:       Console.WriteLine("exception " + Ex.ToString());
 9:     }
10:     catch(DivideByZeroException divEx)
11:     {
12:       Console.WriteLine("never going to see that");
13:     }
```

The compiler will catch the glitch and report an error similar to this one:

```
wrongcatch.cs(10,9): error CS0160: A previous catch clause already
catches all exceptions of this or a super type ('System.Exception')
```

Finally, I have to report one shortcoming (or difference) of NGWS runtime exceptions as compared to SEH: There is no equivalent to the EXCEPTION_CONTINUE_EXECUTION identifier, which is available in SEH exception filters. Basically, EXCEPTION_CONTINUE_EXECUTION enables you to re-execute the piece of code that is responsible for the exception. You had the chance to change variables or the like before the re-execution. My personal favorite technique was performing memory allocation on demand by using access violation exceptions.

Throwing Exceptions

When you have to catch exceptions, someone else must be able to throw them in the first place. And, not only is someone else capable of throwing, you can be in charge, too. It is pretty simple:

```
throw new ArgumentException("Argument can't be 5");
```

All you need is the throw statement and an appropriate exception class. I have picked an exception from the list provided in Table 7.1 for this example.

Table 7.1   Standard Exceptions Provided by the Runtime

Exception Type	Description
Exception	Base class for all exception objects
SystemException	Base class for all errors generated during runtime
IndexOutOfRangeException	Thrown during runtime when an array index is out of range
NullReferenceException	Raised by the runtime when a null object is referenced
InvalidOperationException	Thrown by certain methods when the call to the method is invalid for the object's current state
ArgumentException	Base class of all argument exceptions
ArgumentNullException	Thrown by methods in case an argument is null where not allowed
ArgumentOutOfRangeException	Thrown by a method when an argument is not within a given range
InteropException	Base class for exceptions that are targeted at or occur in environments outside the NGWS runtime
ComException	Exception containing COM classic's HRESULT information
SEHException	Exception encapsulating Win32 structured exception-handling information

However, you need not create a new exception when you already have one at your disposal inside a catch statement. Maybe none of the exceptions in Table 7.1 fits your special needs—why not create a new type of exception? Both topics are covered in the upcoming sections.

Re-Throwing Exceptions

While you are inside a catch statement, you can decide to throw the exception you are currently handling again, leaving further handling to some outer try-catch statement. An example of this approach is shown in Listing 7.8.

Listing 7.8   Throwing an Exception Again

```
1:      try
2:      {
3:        checked
4:        {
5:          for (;nCurDig <= nComputeTo; nCurDig++)
6:            nFactorial *= nCurDig;
7:        }
8:      }
9:      catch (OverflowException oe)
10:     {
11:       Console.WriteLine("Computing {0} caused an overflow
          ➥exception", nComputeTo);
12:       throw;
13:     }
```

Note that I do not need to specify the exception variable I have declared. Although it is optional, you could also write

```
throw oe;
```

Now someone else has to take care of this exception!

Creating Your Own Exception Class

Although it is recommended that you use the predefined exception classes, for programmatic scenarios it can be handy to create your own exception classes. Creating your own exception class enables customers of your exception class to take a different action based on that very exception class.

The exception class MyImportantException presented in Listing 7.9 follows two rules: First, it ends the class name with Exception. Second, it implements all three recommended common constructors. You should abide by these rules, too.

Listing 7.9   Implementing Your Own Exception Class
                MyImportantException

```
 1: using System;
 2:
 3: public class MyImportantException:Exception
 4: {
 5:   public MyImportantException()
 6:     :base() {}
 7:
 8:   public MyImportantException(string message)
 9:     :base(message) {}
10:
11:   public MyImportantException(string message, Exception inner)
12:     :base(message,inner) {}
13: }
14:
15: public class ExceptionTestApp
16: {
17:   public static void TestThrow()
18:   {
19:     throw new MyImportantException("something bad has
        ➥happened.");
20:   }
21:
22:   public static void Main()
23:   {
24:     try
25:     {
26:       ExceptionTestApp.TestThrow();
27:     }
28:     catch (Exception e)
29:     {
30:       Console.WriteLine(e);
31:     }
32:   }
33: }
```

As you can see, the MyImportantException exception class does not implement any special features, but is based entirely on the

`System.Exception` class. The remainder of the program then tests the new exception class, using a `catch` statement for the `System.Exception` class.

If there is no special implementation other than three constructors for `MyImportantException`, what is the point of creating it? It is the type that is important—you can use it in a `catch` statement instead of a more general exception class. A client of code that might throw your new exception can react with specific `catch` code.

When programming a class library with your own namespace, place your exceptions in that namespace, too. Although it is not presented in this example, you should extend your exception classes with appropriate properties for extended error information.

Do's and Donts of Exception Handling

As a final word of advice, here is a list of Do's and Donts for exception throwing and handling:

- Do provide a meaningful text when throwing the exception.

- Do throw exceptions only when the condition is really exceptional; that is, when a normal return value is not sufficient.

- Do throw an `ArgumentException` if your method or property is passed bad parameters.

- Do throw an `InvalidOperationException` when the invoked operation is not appropriate for the object's current state.

- Do throw the most appropriate exception.

- Do use chained exceptions. They enable you to trace the exception tree.

- Don't use exceptions for normal or expected errors.

- Don't use exceptions for normal control of flow.

- Don't throw `NullReferenceException` or `IndexOutOfRangeException` in methods.

Summary

This chapter started by introducing you to overflow checking. You can enable or disable overflow checking for your entire C# application by using a compiler switch (the default is off). If you need finer control, you can use the checked and unchecked statements, which enable you to execute a block of statements either with or without overflow checking, regardless of the compiler settings for the application.

When an overflow occurs, an exception is raised. How that exception is handled is up to you. I presented various approaches, including the one you are most likely to use throughout your applications: employing try, catch, and finally statements. Along with various examples, you learned differences to the structured exception handling (SEH) of WIN32.

Handling exceptions is for users of classes; however, if you are in charge of creating new classes, you can throw exceptions. You have multiple choices: throwing the exceptions you already caught, throwing existing framework exceptions, or creating new exception classes that are specific for the programmatic purpose.

Finally, you had a required reading of various Do's and Donts for the throwing and handling of exceptions.

CHAPTER 8

Writing Components in C#

- Your First Component
- Working with Namespaces

This chapter is about writing components in C#. You learn how to write a component, how to compile it, and how to use it in a client application. A further step down the road is using namespaces to organize your applications.

The chapter is structured into two major sections:

- Your first component
- Working with namespaces

Your First Component

The examples presented so far in this book used a class immediately in the same application. The class and its consumer were contained in the same executable. Now we will split class and consumer into a component and a client, respectively, which are then located in different binaries (executables).

Although you still create a DLL for the component, the approach itself is quite different from writing a COM component in C++. You have much less infrastructure to deal with. The following sections show you how to build a component and the client that uses it:

- Building the component
- Compiling the component
- Creating a simple client application

Building the Component

Because I am a fan of useable examples, I decided to create a Web-related class that might come in handy for many of you: it retrieves a Web page from a server and stores that page in a string variable for later reuse. And all this happens with the help of the NGWS framework.

The class's name is RequestWebPage; it has two constructors—one property and one method. The property is named URL, and it stores the Web address of the page that is to be retrieved by the method GetContent. This method does all the work for you (see Listing 8.1).

Listing 8.1   The RequestWebPage *Class for Retrieving HTML Pages from Web Servers*

```
1: using System;
2: using System.Net;
3: using System.IO;
4: using System.Text;
5:
6: public class RequestWebPage
7: {
8:   private const int BUFFER_SIZE = 128;
```

```
 9:    private string m_strURL;
10:
11:    public RequestWebPage()
12:    {
13:    }
14:
15:    public RequestWebPage(string strURL)
16:    {
17:      m_strURL = strURL;
18:    }
19:
20:    public string URL
21:    {
22:      get { return m_strURL;  }
23:      set { m_strURL = value; }
24:    }
25:    public void GetContent(out string strContent)
26:    {
27:      // check the URL
28:      if (m_strURL == "")
29:        throw new ArgumentException("URL must be provided.");
30:
31:    WebRequest theRequest = (WebRequest)
       ➥WebRequestFactory.Create(m_strURL);
32:      WebResponse theResponse = theRequest.GetResponse();
33:
34:      // set up the byte buffer for the response
35:      int BytesRead = 0;
36:      Byte[] Buffer = new Byte[BUFFER_SIZE];
37:
38:      Stream ResponseStream = theResponse.GetResponseStream();
39:      BytesRead = ResponseStream.Read(Buffer, 0, BUFFER_SIZE);
40:
41:      // use StringBuilder to speed up the allocation process
42:      StringBuilder strResponse = new StringBuilder("");
43:      while (BytesRead != 0 )
44:      {
45:        strResponse.Append(Encoding.ASCII.GetString(Buffer,
           ➥0,BytesRead));
46:        BytesRead = ResponseStream.Read(Buffer, 0, BUFFER_SIZE);
47:      }
48:
49:      // assign the out parameter
50:      strContent = strResponse.ToString();
51:  }
52: }
```

I could have done this with the parameterless constructor, but I decided that initializing URL in the constructor might be useful. When I decide to change the URL later—for retrieving a second page, for example—it is exposed via get and set accessors of the URL property.

The fun begins in the GetContent method. First, the code performs a really simple check on the URL, and if it is not appropriate, an ArgumentException is thrown. After that, I ask the WebRequestFactory to create a new WebRequest object based on the URL I pass to it.

Because I do not want to send cookies, additional headers, query strings, or the like, I access the WebResponse immediately (line 32). If you need any of the aforementioned features for the request, you must implement them before this line.

Lines 35 and 36 initialize a byte buffer that is used to read data from the response stream. Ignoring the StringBuilder class for the moment, the while loop simply iterates as long as there is still some data left to read from the response stream. The last read operation would return zero, thus terminating the loop.

Now I want to come back to the StringBuilder class. Why do I use an instance of this class instead of simply concatenating the byte buffer to a string variable? Look at the following example:

```
strMyString = strMyString + "some more text";
```

Here, it is clear that you are copying values. The constant "some more text" is boxed in a string variable, and a new string variable is created based on the addition operation. This is then finally assigned to strMyString. That's a lot of copying, isn't it?

But you can argue that

```
strMyString += "some more text";
```

does not exhibit this behavior. Sorry, that's the wrong answer for C#. It behaves exactly the same as the described assignment operation.

The way out of this problem is to use the `StringBuilder` class. It works with one buffer, and you perform append, insert, remove, and replace operations without incurring the copy behavior I have described. That is why I used it in this class to concatenate the content that is read from the buffer.

The buffer brings me to the last important piece of code in this class—the encoding conversion of line 45. It simply takes care that I get the character set I am asking for.

Finally, when all content is read and converted, I explicitly request a string object from the `StringBuilder` and assign it to the `out` variable. A return value would have incurred yet another copy operation.

Compiling the Component

The work you have done so far isn't different from writing a class inside a normal application. What makes it different is the compilation process. You have to create a library instead of an application:

```
csc /r:System.Net.dll /t:library /out:wrq.dll webrequest.cs
```

The compiler switch `/t:library` tells the C# compiler to create a library and not to search for a static `Main` method. Also, because I am using the `System.Net` namespace, I have to reference (`/r:`) its library, which is `System.Net.dll`.

Your library named `wrq.dll` is now ready to be used in a client application. Because we work only with private components in this chapter, you do not need to copy the library to a special location other than the client application's directory.

Creating a Simple Client Application

When the component is written and successfully compiled, all you have to do is to use it in a client application. I once again have created a simple command-line application, which retrieves the start page of a development site I maintain (see Listing 8.2).

Listing 8.2   Using the `RequestWebPage` *Class to Retrieve a*
Simple Page

```
 1: using System;
 2:
 3: class TestWebReq
 4: {
 5:   public static void Main()
 6:   {
 7:      RequestWebPage wrq = new RequestWebPage();
 8:      wrq.URL = "http://www.alphasierrapapa.com/iisdev/";
 9:
10:      string strResult;
11:      try
12:      {
13:        wrq.GetContent(out strResult);
14:      }
15:      catch (Exception e)
16:      {
17:        Console.WriteLine(e);
18:        return;
19:      }
20:
21:      Console.WriteLine(strResult);
22:   }
23: }
```

Notice that I have enclosed the call to `GetContent` in a `try catch`
statement. One reason for this is because `GetContent` could throw an
`ArgumentException` exception. Furthermore, the NGWS framework
classes I call inside the component could also throw exceptions. Because
I do not handle these exceptions inside the class, I have to handle them
here.

The remainder of the code is nothing more than straightforward
component use—calling the standard constructor, accessing a property,
and executing a method. But wait: You need to pay attention when
compiling the application. You have to tell the compiler to reference your
new component's library DLL:

```
csc /r:wrq.dll wrclient.cs
```

Now you are all set and can test the application. Output will scroll by, but you can see that the application works. You could also add code to parse the returned HTML using regular expressions, and extract information to your liking. I envision the use of an SSL-modified version of this class for online credit card verification in ASP+ pages.

You might have noticed that there is no special using statement for the library you created. The reason is that you didn't define a namespace in the component's source file.

Working with Namespaces

You have already often used namespaces, such as System and System.Net. C# uses namespaces to organize programs, and the hierarchical nature of the organization makes it easy to present elements of a program to other programs. Even if they are not used for external presentation, namespaces are a good way of internally organizing your applications.

Although it is not mandatory, you always should create namespaces to identify the hierarchy of your application clearly. The NGWS framework should give you a good idea of how to build such a hierarchy.

The following code snippet shows the simple namespace My.Test (the dot denotes a hierarchy level) declaration in a C# source file:

```
namespace My.Test
{
    // anything in here belongs to the namespace
}
```

When you access an element in the namespace, you either have to fully qualify it with the namespace identifier, or use the using directive to import all elements into your current namespace. Previous examples in this book demonstrated how to employ these techniques.

Before you begin using namespaces, just a few words on access security: If you do not add a specific access modifier, all types will be internal by default. Use public when you want the type to be accessible from outside. No other modifiers are allowed.

That is enough theory about namespaces. Let's proceed to implementing that theory—the following sections show how to use namespaces when building component applications:

- Wrapping a class in a namespace

- Using namespaces in your client application

- Adding multiple classes to a namespace

Wrapping a Class in a Namespace

Now that you know what a namespace is in theory, let's implement one in real life. A natural choice for the namespace in this and upcoming examples is `Presenting.CSharp`. To not bore you with just wrapping the `RequestWebPage` class into it, I decided to write a class for a `Whois` lookup (see Listing 8.3).

*Listing 8.3   Implementing the `WhoisLookup` Class Inside a
            Namespace*

```
 1: using System;
 2: using System.Net.Sockets;
 3: using System.IO;
 4: using System.Text;
 5:
 6: namespace Presenting.CSharp
 7: {
 8:  public class WhoisLookup
 9:  {
10:   public static bool Query(string strDomain, out string
       ➥strWhoisInfo)
11:   {
12:    const int BUFFER_SIZE = 128;
13:
14:    if ("" == strDomain)
15:     throw new ArgumentException("You must specify a domain
        ➥name.");
16:
17:    TCPClient tcpc = new TCPClient();
18:    strWhoisInfo = "N/A";
19:
20:    // try to connect to the whois server
```

```
21:      if (tcpc.Connect("whois.networksolutions.com", 43) != 0)
22:          return false;
23:
24:      // get the stream
25:      Stream s = tcpc.GetStream();
26:
27:      // send the request
28:      strDomain += "\r\n";
29:      Byte[] bDomArr =
        ➥Encoding.ASCII.GetBytes(strDomain.ToCharArray());
30:      s.Write(bDomArr, 0, strDomain.Length);
31:
32:      Byte[] Buffer = new Byte[BUFFER_SIZE];
33:      StringBuilder strWhoisResponse = new StringBuilder("");
34:
35:      int BytesRead = s.Read(Buffer, 0, BUFFER_SIZE);
36:      while (BytesRead != 0 )
37:      {
38:       strWhoisResponse.Append(Encoding.ASCII.GetString(Buffer,
        ➥0,BytesRead));
39:       BytesRead = s.Read(Buffer, 0, BUFFER_SIZE);
40:      }
41:
42:      tcpc.Close();
43:      strWhoisInfo = strWhoisResponse.ToString();
44:      return true;
45:    }
46:  }
47: }
```

The namespace is declared in line 6, and it encloses the WhoisLookup class with the angle brackets in lines 7 and 47. That's really all you have to do to declare your own new namespace.

The class WhoisLookup has, of course, some interesting code in it, especially because it shows how easy socket programming is in C#. After the not-so-stellar domain name check in the static Query method, I instantiate an object of type TCPClient, which is used to perform all communications on port 43 with the Whois server. The connection to the server is established in line 21:

```
if (tcpc.Connect("whois.networksolutions.com", 43) != 0)
```

Because a failed connection attempt is an expected result, this method does not throw an exception. (Do you still remember the Do's and Donts of exception handling?) The return value is an error code, and zero indicates connection success.

For a Whois lookup, I must first send some information—the domain name I want to look up—to the server. To achieve this, I first obtain a reference to the bidirectional stream of the current TCP connection (line 25). I then append a carriage return/linefeed pair to the domain name to denote the end of my query. Repackaged in a byte array, I send the request to the Whois server (line 30).

The remainder of the code is very similar to the `RequestWebPage` class in that I again use a buffer to read the response from the remote server. When the buffer is finished reading, the connection is closed, and the retrieved response is returned to the caller. The reason I explicitly call the `Close` method is that I do not want to wait for the garbage collector to destroy the connection. Never hang on too long to scarce resources such as TCP ports.

Before you can use the class in an NGWS component, you must compile it as a library. Although there's now a namespace defined, the compilation command hasn't changed:

```
csc /r:System.Net.dll /t:library /out:whois.dll whois.cs
```

Note that it isn't necessary to specify the `/out:` switch if you want the library to be named the same way as the original C# source file. It is just a good habit to specify the switch because most projects won't consist of a single source file. If you specify multiple source files, the library is named after the first source file in the list.

Using Namespaces in Your Client Application

Because you developed your component with a namespace, the client either has to import the namespace

```
using Presenting.CSharp;
```

or use fully qualified names for the elements in the namespace, such as

```
Presenting.CSharp.WhoisLookup.Query(...);
```

If you don't have to expect conflicts between the elements in the namespaces you want to import, the using directive is preferred, especially because you have less to type. A sample client program using the component is implemented in Listing 8.4.

Listing 8.4 Testing the WhoisLookup Component

```
1: using System;
2: using Presenting.CSharp;
3:
4: class TestWhois
5: {
6:   public static void Main()
7:   {
8:     string strResult;
9:     bool bReturnValue;
10:
11:     try
12:     {
13:       bReturnValue = WhoisLookup.Query("microsoft.com", out
          ➥strResult);
14:     }
15:     catch (Exception e)
16:     {
17:       Console.WriteLine(e);
18:       return;
19:     }
20:     if (bReturnValue)
21:       Console.WriteLine(strResult);
22:     else
23:       Console.WriteLine("Could not obtain information from
          ➥server.");
24:   }
25: }
```

Line 2 imports the Presenting.CSharp namespace with the using directive. Whenever I reference the WhoisLookup class now, I can omit the namespace part of the fully qualified name.

The program itself performs a Whois lookup for the microsoft.com domain—you can replace microsoft.com with your own domain name. You could make the client even more useful by allowing the domain name to be passed via a command-line parameter. Listing 8.5 implements that functionality, but it doesn't implement proper exception handling (to make the listing shorter).

*Listing 8.5   Passing the Command-Line Argument to the Query
          Method*

```
 1: using System;
 2: using Presenting.CSharp;
 3:
 4: class WhoisShort
 5: {
 6:   public static void Main(string[] args)
 7:   {
 8:     string strResult;
 9:     bool bReturnValue;
10:
11:     bReturnValue = WhoisLookup.Query(args[0], out strResult);
12:
13:     if (bReturnValue)
14:       Console.WriteLine(strResult);
15:     else
16:       Console.WriteLine("Lookup failed.");
17:   }
18: }
```

All you have to do is compile this application:

```
csc /r:whois.dll whoisclnt.cs
```

You then can execute the application with a command-line parameter. For
example, to execute with `microsoft.com`

```
whoisclnt microsoft.com
```

When the query runs successfully, you are presented with the registration
information for microsoft.com. (An abbreviated version of the output is
shown in Listing 8.6.) This is a handy little application, written with a
componentized approach, in less than an hour. How long would it have
taken to write in C++? Luckily, I can no longer recall how long it took
me when I did it for the first time.

Listing 8.6   Whois Information About microsoft.com (Abbreviated)

```
D:\CSharp\Samples\Namespace>whoisclient
...


Registrant:
Microsoft Corporation (MICROSOFT-DOM)
   1 microsoft way
   redmond, WA 98052
   US


   Domain Name: MICROSOFT.COM


   Administrative Contact:
      Microsoft Hostmaster  (MH37-ORG)  msnhst@MICROSOFT.COM
   Technical Contact, Zone Contact:
      MSN NOC  (MN5-ORG)  msnnoc@MICROSOFT.COM
   Billing Contact:
      Microsoft-Internic Billing Issues  (MDB-ORG)
      msnbill@MICROSOFT.COM


   Record last updated on 20-May-2000.
   Record expires on 03-May-2010.
   Record created on 02-May-1991.
   Database last updated on 9-Jun-2000 13:50:52 EDT.


   Domain servers in listed order:


   ATBD.MICROSOFT.COM          131.107.1.7
   DNS1.MICROSOFT.COM          131.107.1.240
   DNS4.CP.MSFT.NET            207.46.138.11
   DNS5.CP.MSFT.NET            207.46.138.12
```

Adding Multiple Classes to a Namespace

It would be nice to have both the WhoisLookup and the RequestWebPage
class in a single namespace. WhoisLookup is already part of the
namespace, so you only have to make the RequestWebPage class part of
the namespace, too.

The necessary changes are applied easily. You only have to wrap the RequestWebPage class with the namespace:

```
namespace Presenting.CSharp
{
public class RequestWebPage
{
...
}
}
```

Although the two classes are contained in two different files, they are part of the same namespace after compilation:

```
csc /r:System.Net.dll /t:library /out:presenting.csharp.dll
➡whois.cs webrequest.cs
```

You are not required to name the DLL after the exact namespace name. However, doing so helps you to remember more easily which libraries to reference when compiling client applications.

Summary

In this chapter, you learned how to build a component that can be used in a client application. At first, you didn't care about namespaces, but this feature was introduced later with a second component. Namespaces are a great way to organize your applications both internally and externally.

Components in C# can be built very easily, and you don't even need to perform a special installation as long as the library resides in the same directory as the application. When creating class libraries that must be used by multiple clients, this picture changes a bit—and the next chapter will tell you why.

CHAPTER 9

Configuration and Deployment

- Conditional Compilation
- Documentation Comments in XML
- Versioning Your Code

In the last chapter, you learned how to create a component, and how to use it in a simple test application. Although the component would be ready to ship, you should also consider one of the following techniques:

- Conditional compilation
- Documentation comments
- Versioning your code

Conditional Compilation

A feature I couldn't live without is conditional compilation of my code. Conditional compilation enables me to exclude or include code based on certain conditions; for example, to build a debug version, demo version, or retail version of my application. Examples of code that might be included or excluded are licensing code, nag screens, or whatever you can come up with.

In C#, there are two ways to perform conditional compilation:

- Preprocessor usage
- The conditional attribute

Preprocessor Usage

In C++, the preprocessor is a separate step before the compiler starts compiling your code. In C#, the preprocessor is "emulated" by the compiler itself—there is no separate preprocessor. It is simply conditional compilation.

Although the C# compiler does not support macros, you have the necessary features for conditional exclusion and inclusion of code based on the definitions of symbols. The following sections introduce you to the various directives that are supported in C#, which are quite similar to the ones found in C++:

- Defining symbols
- Excluding code based on symbols
- Raising errors and warnings

Defining Symbols

You cannot create macros with the preprocessor that comes with the C# compiler; however, you still can define symbols. These symbols are used to exclude or include code depending on whether or not a certain symbol is defined.

The first way to define a symbol is to use the `#define` directive in a C# source file:

```
#define DEBUG
```

This defines the symbol `DEBUG`, and its scope is the file it is defined in. Please note that the definition of a symbol must occur before any other statements. For example, the following piece of code is incorrect:

```
using System;
#define DEBUG
```

The compiler will flag the preceding code as an error. You can also use the compiler to define symbols (global to all files):

```
csc /define:DEBUG mysymbols.cs
```

If you want to define multiple symbols by using the compiler, you only need to separate them with a semicolon:

```
csc /define:RELEASE;DEMOVERSION mysymbols.cs
```

In a C# source file, the definition for these two symbols would simply be two separate lines of `#define` directives.

Sometimes you might want to undefine a certain symbol in a source file (of a larger project, for example). You can do this by using the `#undef` directive:

```
#undef DEBUG
```

The rules of `#define` also apply to `#undef`: Its scope is the file in which it is defined, and it must appear before any statements, such as `using`, for example.

That is all there is to know about defining and undefining symbols with the C# preprocessor. The following sections show how to use the symbols to conditionally compile your code.

Including and Excluding Code Based on Symbols

The foremost purpose of symbols is the conditional inclusion or exclusion of code based on whether or not the symbol is defined.

Listing 9.1 contains source code you've already seen, but this time it is conditionally compiled based on a symbol.

Listing 9.1   Conditionally Including Code Using the #if Directive

```
 1: using System;
 2:
 3: public class SquareSample
 4: {
 5:   public void CalcSquare(int nSideLength, out int nSquared)
 6:   {
 7:     nSquared = nSideLength * nSideLength;
 8:   }
 9:
10:   public int CalcSquare(int nSideLength)
11:   {
12:     return nSideLength*nSideLength;
13:   }
14: }
15:
16: class SquareApp
17: {
18:   public static void Main()
19:   {
20:     SquareSample sq = new SquareSample();
21:
22:     int nSquared = 0;
23:
24: #if CALC_W_OUT_PARAM
25:     sq.CalcSquare(20, out nSquared);
26: #else
27:     nSquared = sq.CalcSquare(15);
28: #endif
29:     Console.WriteLine(nSquared.ToString());
30:   }
31: }
```

Note that no symbol is defined in this source file. The symbol is defined (or not) when compiling the application:

```
csc /define:CALC_W_OUT_PARAM square.cs
```

Based on the symbol definition, a different CalcSquare method is called. The emulated preprocessor directives used to evaluate the symbol are

#if, #else, and #endif. They act the same as their C# counterpart, the if statement. You can also use logical AND (&&), logical OR (||), as well as negation (!). An example of this is shown in Listing 9.2.

Listing 9.2 Using #elif to Create Multiple Branches in an #if Directive

```
1: // #define DEBUG
2: #define RELEASE
3: #define DEMOVERSION
4:
5: #if DEBUG
6:    #undef DEMOVERSION
7: #endif
8:
9: using System;
10:
11: class Demo
12: {
13:    public static void Main()
14:    {
15: #if DEBUG
16:       Console.WriteLine("Debug version");
17: #elif RELEASE && !DEMOVERSION
18:       Console.WriteLine("Full release version");
19: #else
20:       Console.WriteLine("Demo version");
21: #endif
22:    }
23: }
```

In this example, all symbols are defined in the C# source file. Note the addition of the #undef statement in line 6. Because I don't compile demo versions of my debug code (an arbitrary choice), I make sure that it wasn't inadvertently defined by someone and undefine it always when DEBUG is defined.

The preprocessor symbols are then used in lines 15–21 to include varying code. Note the use of the #elif directive, which enables you to add multiple branches to the #if directive. This code uses the logical operator && and the negation operator !. It is also possible to use the logical operator ||, as well as equality and inequality operators.

Raising Errors and Warnings

Another possible use of preprocessor directives is to raise compiler errors or warnings depending on certain symbols (or none at all, if you so decide). The respective directives are #warning and #error, and Listing 9.3 demonstrates how to use them in your code.

Listing 9.3   Creating Compiler Warnings and Errors Using Preprocessor Directives

```
1: #define DEBUG
2: #define RELEASE
3: #define DEMOVERSION
4:
5: #if DEMOVERSION && !DEBUG
6:   #warning You are building a demo version
7: #endif
8:
9: #if DEBUG && DEMOVERSION
10:   #error You cannot build a debug demo version
11: #endif
12:
13: using System;
14:
15: class Demo
16: {
17:   public static void Main()
18:   {
19:     Console.WriteLine("Demo application");
20:   }
21: }
```

In this example, a compiler warning is issued when you build a demo version that is not also a debug version (lines 5–7). An error is raised—which prevents generation of the executable—when you try to build a debug demo version. In contrast to the previous example, which simply undefined the offending symbol, this code tells you that what you tried to do is considered an error. This is definitely the better behavior.

The *conditional* Attribute

The preprocessor of C++ is perhaps most often used for defining macros that resolve to a function call in one build, and resolve to nothing in another build. Examples of this include the ASSERT and TRACE macros, which evaluate to function calls when the DEBUG symbol is defined and evaluate to nothing when a release version is built.

With the knowledge that macros are not supported, you might also guess that conditional functionality is dead. Happily, I can report that is not the case. You can include methods based on certain defined symbols by using the conditional attribute:

```
[conditional("DEBUG")]
    public void SomeMethod() { }
```

This method is added to resulting executable only when the symbol DEBUG is defined. And a call to it, such as

```
SomeMethod();
```

is also discarded by the compiler when the method is not included. The functionality is basically the same as with C++ conditional macros.

Before starting an example, I want to point out that the conditional method must have a return type of void. No other return types are allowed. However, you can pass any parameters you want to use.

The example in Listing 9.4 demonstrates how to use the conditional attribute to rebuild the functionality of the TRACE macros found in C++. For simplicity, the output is directed to the console. You could direct it anywhere you want, including a file.

Listing 9.4   Implementing Methods Using the conditional *Attribute*

```
 1: #define DEBUG
 2:
 3: using System;
 4:
 5: class Info
 6: {
 7:    [conditional("DEBUG")]
 8:    public static void Trace(string strMessage)
 9:    {
10:      Console.WriteLine(strMessage);
11:    }
12:
```

continues

Listing 9.4   continued

```
13:    [conditional("DEBUG")]
14:    public static void TraceX(string strFormat,params object[] list)
15:    {
16:       Console.WriteLine(strFormat, list);
17:    }
18: }
19:
20: class TestConditional
21: {
22:    public static void Main()
23:    {
24:       Info.Trace("Cool!");
25:       Info.TraceX("{0} {1} {2}","C", "U", 2001);
26:    }
27: }
```

There are two static methods in the class Info that are conditionally compiled based on the DEBUG symbol: Trace, which takes one parameter, and TraceX, which takes *n* parameters. Implementation of Trace is straightforward. However, TraceX implements a keyword you haven't seen before: params.

The params keyword enables you to specify a method parameter that actually takes any number of arguments. It is similar to the C/C++ ellipsis argument. Note that it must be the last parameter of a method call, and that you can use it only once in the parameter list. After all, these two limitations are pretty obvious.

The intention of using the params keyword is to have a Trace method that can take a format string and an unlimited number of replacement objects. Luckily, there is also a WriteLine method that supports a format string and an object array (line 16).

Which output this little program generates depends entirely on whether the DEBUG symbol is defined. When the DEBUG symbol is defined, both methods are compiled and executed. If DEBUG is not defined, the calls to Trace and TraceX are removed along with their definitions.

Conditional methods are a really powerful means for adding conditional functionality to your applications and components. With a few twists, you can build conditional methods based on multiple symbols linked with logical OR (||) as well as logical AND (&&). For those cases, however, I want to refer you to the C# documentation.

Documentation Comments in XML

A task many programmers do not like at all is writing, which includes comments and documentation. With C#, however, there is a good reason to change your old habits: You can automatically build the documentation from the comments in your code.

The output that is generated by the compiler is pure XML. It can be used as input for the documentation of your component, as well as for tools that use it to display help and tag insight about your component. Visual Studio 7 is such a tool, for example. Good documentation becomes the selling argument it always should have been.

This section is dedicated to showing you how to best use the documentation feature of C#. The examples are extensive, so you don't have the excuse that it was too complicated to figure out how to add the documentation comments. Documentation is an extremely important part of software, especially of components that are to be used by other developers.

In the following sections, the documentation comments are shown for the RequestWebPage class. I have divided the explanation into the following sections:

- Describing an element
- Adding remarks and lists
- Providing examples
- Describing parameters
- Describing properties
- Compiling the documentation

Describing an Element

A first step is to add a simple description to an element. You can do that by using the <summary> tag:

```
/// <summary>This is .... </summary>
```

Every documentation comment starts with a triple forward-slash ///. You place the documentation comment before the element that you want to describe:

```
/// <summary>Class to tear a Webpage from a Webserver</summary>
public class RequestWebPage
```

You can add paragraphs to the description by using the <para> and </para> tags. References to other elements are added using the <see> tag:

```
///    <para>Included in the <see cref="RequestWebPage"/> class</para>
```

This adds a link to the description of the RequestWebPage class. Note that the syntax for the tags is XML syntax, which means that the tags' capitalization matters, and that tags must be nested correctly.

Another interesting tag when documenting an element is the <seealso> tag. It enables you to describe other topics that might be of interest to the reader:

```
/// <seealso cref="System.Net"/>
```

The preceding example tells the reader that he might also want to look up the documentation of the System.Net namespace. You have to always specify the fully qualified name for items outside the current scope.

As promised, Listing 9.5 contains a full example of documentation at work in the RequestWebPage class. Take a look at how tags can be used and nested to generate documentation for a component.

Listing 9.5   Describing an Element Using <summary>, <see>, <para>,
and <seealso> *Tags*

```
 1: using System;
 2: using System.Net;
 3: using System.IO;
 4: using System.Text;
 5:
 6: /// <summary>Class to tear a Webpage from a Webserver</summary>
 7: public class RequestWebPage
 8: {
 9:   private const int BUFFER_SIZE = 128;
10:
11:   /// <summary>m_strURL stores the URL of the Webpage</summary>
12:   private string m_strURL;
13:
14:   /// <summary>RequestWebPage() is the constructor for the class
15:   /// <see cref="RequestWebPage"/> when called without
➥arguments.</summary>
16:   public RequestWebPage()
17:   {
18:   }
19:
20: /// <summary>RequestWebPage(string strURL) is the constructor for
➥the class
21:   ///   <see cref="RequestWebPage"/> when called with an URL as
➥parameter.</summary>
22:   public RequestWebPage(string strURL)
23:   {
24:     m_strURL = strURL;
25:   }
26:
27:   public string URL
28:   {
29:     get { return m_strURL;  }
30:     set { m_strURL = value; }
31:   }
32:
33:   /// <summary>The GetContent(out string strContent) method:
34:   ///    <para>Included in the <see cref="RequestWebPage"/>
➥class</para>
35:   ///    <para>Uses variable <see cref="m_strURL"/></para>
36:   ///      <para>Used to retrieve the content of a Webpage. The URL
```

continues

Listing 9.5 continued

```
37:  ///    of the Webpage (including http://) must already be
38:  ///    stored in the private variable m_strURL.
39:  ///    To do so, call the constructor of the RequestWebPage
40:  ///    class, or set its property <see cref="URL"/> to the
➥URL string.</para>
41:  /// </summary>
42:  /// <seealso cref="System.Net"/>
43:  /// <seealso cref="System.Net.WebResponse"/>
44:  /// <seealso cref="System.Net.WebRequest"/>
45:  /// <seealso cref="System.Net.WebRequestFactory"/>
46:  /// <seealso cref="System.IO.Stream"/>
47:  /// <seealso cref="System.Text.StringBuilder"/>
48:  /// <seealso cref="System.ArgumentException"/>
49:
50:  public bool GetContent(out string strContent)
51:  {
52:    strContent = "";
53:    // ...
54:    return true;
55:  }
56: }
```

Adding Remarks and Lists

The <remarks> tag is where you should specify the bulk of your documentation. This is in contrast to <summary>, where you should specify only a brief description of the element.

You are not limited to supplying paragraph text only (using the <para> tag). For example, you can include bulleted (and even numbered) lists in the remarks section:

```
///    <list type="bullet">
///      <item>Constructor
///        <see cref="RequestWebPage()"/> or
///        <see cref="RequestWebPage(string)"/>
///      </item>
///    </list>
```

This list has one item, and the item references two different constructor descriptions. You are free to add as much content to a list item as you want.

Another tag that is good to use in the remarks section is <paramref>. For example, you can use <paramref> to reference and describe a parameter that is passed to a constructor:

```
/// <remarks>Stores the URL from the parameter
/// <paramref name="strURL"/> in
/// the private variable <see cref="m_strURL"/>.</remarks>
public RequestWebPage(string strURL)
```

You can see all these tags, as well as the previous ones, in action in Listing 9.6.

Listing 9.6   *Adding Remarks and Bulleted Lists to the Documentation*

```
 1: using System;
 2: using System.Net;
 3: using System.IO;
 4: using System.Text;
 5:
 6: /// <summary>Class to tear a Webpage from a Webserver</summary>
 7: /// <remarks>The class RequestWebPage provides:
 8: ///    <para>Methods:
 9: ///      <list type="bullet">
10: ///        <item>Constructor
11: ///          <see cref="RequestWebPage()"/> or
12: ///          <see cref="RequestWebPage(string)"/>
13: ///        </item>
14: ///      </list>
15: ///    </para>
16: ///    <para>Properties:
17: ///        <list type="bullet">
18: ///        <item>
19: ///          <see cref="URL"/>
20: ///        </item>
21: ///      </list>
22: ///    </para>
23: /// </remarks>
24: public class RequestWebPage
25: {
```

continues

Listing 9.6   continued

```
26:   private const int BUFFER_SIZE = 128;
27:
28:   /// <summary>m_strURL stores the URL of the Webpage</summary>
29:   private string m_strURL;
30:
31:   /// <summary>RequestWebPage() is the constructor for the class
32:   /// <see cref="RequestWebPage"/> when called without
➥arguments.</summary>
33:   public RequestWebPage()
34:   {
35:   }
36:
37:   /// <summary>RequestWebPage(string strURL) is the constructor
➥for the class
38:   ///    <see cref="RequestWebPage"/> when called with an URL as
➥parameter.</summary>
39:   /// <remarks>Stores the URL from the parameter
➥<paramref name="strURL"/> in
40:   ///    the private variable <see cref="m_strURL"/>.</remarks>
41:   public RequestWebPage(string strURL)
42:   {
43:     m_strURL = strURL;
44:   }
45:
46:   /// <remarks>Sets the value of <see cref="m_strURL"/>.
47:   ///        Returns the value of <see cref="m_strURL"/>.
➥</remarks>
48:   public string URL
49:   {
50:     get { return m_strURL;  }
51:     set { m_strURL = value; }
52:   }
53:
54:   /// <summary>The GetContent(out string strContent) method:
55:   ///    <para>Included in the <see cref="RequestWebPage"/>
➥class</para>
56:   ///    <para>Uses variable <see cref="m_strURL"/></para>
57:   ///     <para>Used to retrieve the content of a Webpage. The URL
58:   ///      of the Webpage (including http://) must already be
59:   ///      stored in the private variable m_strURL.
60:   ///      To do so, call the constructor of the RequestWebPage
61:   ///      class, or set its property <see cref="URL"/>
➥to the URL string.</para>
```

```
62:    /// </summary>
63:    /// <remarks>Retrieves the content of the Webpage specified in
64:    ///    the property<see cref="URL"/> and hands it over to the out
65:    ///    parameter <paramref name="strContent"/>.
66:    ///    The method is implemented using:
67:    ///    <list>
68:    ///       <item>The <see
➥cref="System.Net.WebRequestFactory.Create"/>
➥method.</item>
69:    ///       <item>The <see
➥cref="System.Net.WebRequest.GetResponse"/>
➥method.</item>
70:    ///       <item>The <see
➥cref="System.Net.WebResponse.GetResponseStream"/>
➥method</item>
71:    ///       <item>The <see cref="System.IO.Stream.Read"/>
➥method</item>
72:    ///       <item>The <see
➥cref="System.Text.StringBuilder.Append"/>
➥method</item>
73:    ///       <item>The <see cref="System.Text.Encoding.ASCII"/>
➥property together with its
74:    ///       <see cref="System.Text.Encoding.ASCII.GetString"/>
➥method</item>
75:    ///       <item>The <see cref="System.Object.ToString"/> method
➥for the
76:    ///          <see cref="System.IO.Stream"/> object.</item>
77:    ///    </list>
78:    ///    </remarks>
79:    /// <seealso cref="System.Net"/>
80:    public bool GetContent(out string strContent)
81:    {
82:      strContent = "";
83:      // ...
84:      return true;
85:    }
86: }
```

Providing Examples

There is no better way to document the usage of an object or method than
by providing a good code example. Therefore, it is no wonder that the
documentation comments also have tags for declaring examples:

<example> and <code>. The <example> tag encloses the entire example including the description and code, whereas the <code> tag encloses only (surprise, surprise!) the example's code.

Listing 9.7 shows how to implement code examples. The examples included are for both constructors. You have to provide the example for the GetContent method.

Listing 9.7   Explaining the Concepts Using Examples

```
 1: using System;
 2: using System.Net;
 3: using System.IO;
 4: using System.Text;
 5:
 6: /// <summary>Class to tear a Webpage from a Webserver</summary>
 7: /// <remarks> ... </remarks>
 8: public class RequestWebPage
 9: {
10:   private const int BUFFER_SIZE = 128;
11:
12:   /// <summary>m_strURL stores the URL of the Webpage</summary>
13:   private string m_strURL;
14:
15:   /// <summary>RequestWebPage() is ... </summary>
16:   /// <example>This example shows you how to call the constructor
17:   ///   of the class RequestWebPage() without arguments:
18:   ///   <code>
19:   ///     public class MyClass
20:   ///     {
21:   ///       public static void Main()
22:   ///       {
23:   ///         public
24:   ///         string strContent;
25:   ///         RequestWebPage objRWP = new RequestWebPage();
26:   ///         objRWP.URL = "http://www.alphasierrapapa.com";
27:   ///         objRWP.GetContent(out strContent);
28:   ///         Console.WriteLine(strContent);
29:   ///       }
30:   ///     }
31:   ///   </code>
32:   /// </example>
33:   public RequestWebPage()
34:   {
35:   }
36:
```

```
37:  /// <summary>RequestWebPage(string strURL) is ... </summary>
38:  /// <remarks> ... </remarks>
39:  /// <example>This example shows you how to call
40:  ///  RequestWebPage() with the URL parameter:
41:  ///  <code>
42:  ///  public class MyClass
43:  ///  {
44:  ///   public static void Main()
45:  ///   {
46:  ///    string strContent;
47:  ///    RequestWebPage objRWP = new
➥RequestWebPage("http://www.alphasierrapapa.com");
48:  ///     objRWP.GetContent(out strContent);
49:  ///  Console.WriteLine("\n\nContent of the Webpage "+
➥objRWP.URL+":\n\n");
50:  ///    Console.WriteLine(strContent);
51:  ///   }
52:  ///  }
53:  ///  </code>
54:  /// </example>
55:  public RequestWebPage(string strURL)
56:  {
57:   m_strURL = strURL;
58:  }
59:
60:  /// <remarks> ... </remarks>
61:  public string URL
62:  {
63:   get { return m_strURL;  }
64:   set { m_strURL = value; }
65:  }
66:
67:  /// <summary>The GetContent(out string strContent) method: ...
➥</summary>
68:  /// <remarks> ... </remarks>
69:  /// <seealso cref="System.Net"/>
70:  public bool GetContent(out string strContent)
71:  {
72:   strContent = "";
73:   // ...
74:   return true;
75:  }
76: }
```

Describing Parameters

An important task I have neglected so far is properly describing the parameters of constructors, methods, and the like. But once again, it is pretty straightforward. All you have to do is insert a <param> tag, like this

```
/// <param name="strURL">
/// Used to hand over the URL of the Webpage to the object.
/// Its value is stored in the private variable <see cref="m_strURL"/>.
/// </param>
```

This definition was for a simple in parameter. Note that you could also use <para> inside the <param> tag.

A return parameter is described in a slightly different way:

```
/// <returns>
/// <para>true: Content retrieved</para>
/// <para>false: Content not retrieved</para>
/// </returns>
```

As you can see, a return parameter is described inside the <returns> tag. The complete example of using parameter description is shown in Listing 9.8.

Listing 9.8   Describing Method Parameters and Return Values

```
 1: using System;
 2: using System.Net;
 3: using System.IO;
 4: using System.Text;
 5:
 6: /// <summary>Class to tear a Webpage from a Webserver</summary>
 7: /// <remarks> ... </remarks>
 8: public class RequestWebPage
 9: {
10:   private const int BUFFER_SIZE = 128;
11:
12:   /// <summary>m_strURL stores the URL of the Webpage</summary>
13:   private string m_strURL;
14:
15:   /// <summary>RequestWebPage() is ... </summary>
16:   /// <example>This example ...
17:   ///   <code>
18:   ///     public class MyClass
19:   ///     {
20:   ///       ...
21:   ///     }
22:   ///   </code>
```

```
23:   /// </example>
24:   public RequestWebPage()
25:   {
26:   }
27:
28:   /// <summary>RequestWebPage(string strURL) is ... </summary>
29:   /// <remarks> ... </remarks>
30:   /// <param name="strURL">
31:   ///  Used to hand over the URL of the Webpage to the object.
32:   ///  Its value is stored in the private variable <see
➥cref="m_strURL"/>.
33:   /// </param>
34:   /// <example> ... </example>
35:   public RequestWebPage(string strURL)
36:   {
37:    m_strURL = strURL;
38:   }
39:
40:   /// <remarks> ... </remarks>
41:   public string URL
42:   {
43:    get { return m_strURL;  }
44:    set { m_strURL = value; }
45:   }
46:
47:   /// <summary>The GetContent(out string strContent) method: ...
➥</summary>
48: /// <remarks>Retrieves the content of the Webpage specified in
➥the property
49:   ///  <see cref="URL"/> and hands it over to the out parameter
50:   ///  <paramref name="strContent"/>.
51:   ///  The method is implemented using ...
52:   /// </remarks>
53:   /// <param name="strContent">Returns the Content of the
➥Webpage</param>
54:   /// <returns>
55:   ///  <para>true: Content retrieved</para>
56:   ///  <para>false: Content not retrieved</para>
57:   /// </returns>
58:   /// <seealso cref="System.Net"/>
59:   public bool GetContent(out string strContent)
60:   {
61:    strContent = "";
62:    // ...
63:      return true;
64:   }
65: }
```

Describing Properties

To describe a class's properties, you must use a special tag: the <value> tag. With this tag, you can specifically flag a property, and the <value> tag more or less replaces the <summary> tag.

Listing 9.9 contains a property description for the URL property of the RequestWebPage class (lines 30 and following). Take the time to once again look at the other tags you can use to document your component.

Listing 9.9   Adding Property Descriptions with the <value> Tag

```
 1: using System;
 2: using System.Net;
 3: using System.IO;
 4: using System.Text;
 5:
 6: /// <summary>Class to tear a Webpage from a Webserver</summary>
 7: /// <remarks> ... </remarks>
 8: public class RequestWebPage
 9: {
10:   private const int BUFFER_SIZE = 128;
11:
12:   /// <summary>m_strURL stores the URL of the Webpage</summary>
13:   private string m_strURL;
14:
15:   /// <summary>RequestWebPage() is ... </summary>
16:   /// <example> ... </example>
17:   public RequestWebPage()
18:   {
19:   }
20:
21:   /// <summary>RequestWebPage(string strURL) is ... </summary>
22:   /// <remarks> ... </remarks>
23:   /// <param name="strURL"> ... </param>
24:   /// <example>This example ... </example>
25:   public RequestWebPage(string strURL)
26:   {
27:     m_strURL = strURL;
28:   }
29:
30:   /// <value>The property URL is to get or set the URL for the
➥Webpage </value>
31:   /// <remarks>Sets the value of <see cref="m_strURL"/>.
```

```
32:   ///     Returns the value of <see cref="m_strURL"/>.</remarks>
33:   public string URL
34:   {
35:     get { return m_strURL;  }
36:     set { m_strURL = value; }
37:   }
38:
39:   /// <summary>The GetContent(out string strContent) method: ...
➡</summary>
40:   /// <remarks>Retrieves the content of the Webpage specified in
➡the property
41:   ///   <see cref="URL"/> and hands it over to the out parameter
42:   ///   <paramref name="strContent"/>.
43:   ///   The method is implemented using: ...
44:   /// </remarks>
45:   /// <param name="strContent">Returns the Content of the
➡Webpage</param>
46:   /// <returns>
47:   ///   <para>true: Content retrieved</para>
48:   ///   <para>false: Content not retrieved</para>
49:   /// </returns>
50:   /// <seealso cref="System.Net"/>
51:   public bool GetContent(out string strContent)
52:   {
53:     strContent = "";
54:     // ...
55:     return true;
56:   }
57: }
```

Compiling the Documentation

The documentation process of your component is now complete. You have thoroughly documented your constructors, methods, properties, parameters, and so on. Now you want to create the XML file, based on the documentation remarks in your source code, and be able to ship it to your customers. The good news is that all you have to do is use the compiler switch /doc:

```
csc /r:System.Net.dll /doc:wrq.xml /t:library /out:wrq.dll wrq.cs
```

The compiler switch in question is /doc:docfilename.xml. Given that you didn't make errors in your documentation (yes, it is checked for validity!), you now have an XML file that describes your component.

Instead of showing you the entire XML file as a listing, I want you to open it in Internet Explorer, as shown in Figure 9.1. Using Internet Explorer, you can browse the hierarchy and the information that were generated from your documentation comments.

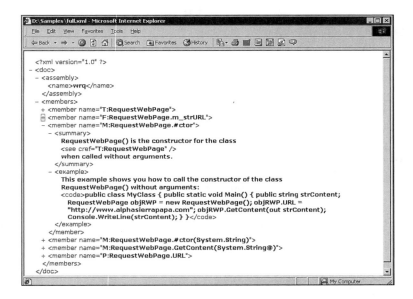

Figure 9.1

Viewing the documentation XML file in Internet Explorer.

Although I do not want to dig too deep into the semantics of the XML file that is generated, I do want to explain how the ID (the member's name attribute) is generated for the elements you have documented. The first part of the ID (before the colon) is determined by the type:

- N—Denotes a namespace.

- T—Identifies a type. This can be class, interface, struct, enum, or delegate.

- F—Describes a field of a class.

- P—Refers to a property, which can also be an indexer or indexed property.

- M—Identifies a method. This includes special methods such as constructors and operators.

- E—Events are denoted by a capital E.

- !—Denotes an error string; provides information about a link that the C# compiler could not resolve.

Following the colon is the fully qualified name of the element, including the root of the namespace, as well as enclosing types. If the element has periods in its name, these are replaced by the hash sign, #. Parameters for methods are enclosed in parentheses, and commas separate the arguments. The element type is encoded by its NGWS signature, and a list of these can be found in the NGWS SDK documentation.

Under normal circumstances, you do not have to care about the preceding XML documentation details. Just create and ship the XML file with your component and users of programming tools will be very happy with your software!

Versioning Your Code

Versioning is a problem that is known today as "DLL Hell." Applications install and use shared components, and one application eventually breaks because it is not compatible with the currently installed version of the component. Shared components today present more problems than they solve.

One of the primary goals of the NGWS runtime is to solve the versioning problem. At center stage of the new approach are the NGWS components (again, this is a term refering to the packaging, not the contents), which enable the developer to specify version dependencies between different pieces of software, and the NGWS runtime enforces those rules at runtime.

I want to introduce you to NGWS components, show what they can be used for, and what differences exist from today's DLLs with regard to versioning.

NGWS Components

Although I didn't specifically call it an NGWS component back then, the first library you compiled was an NGWS component—the C# compiler, by default, always creates NGWS components for your executables. So, what then is an NGWS component?

First of all, an *NGWS component* is the fundamental unit of sharing and reuse in the NGWS runtime. Therefore, versioning is enforced on the component level. An NGWS component also is the boundary for security enforcement, class deployment, and type resolution. An application you build will be typically comprised of multiple NGWS components.

Because we are talking about versioning, what does an NGWS component version number look like? In general, it is comprised of four parts:

```
major version.minor version.build number.revision
```

This version number is called the *compatibility version*. It is used by the class loader to decide which version of an NGWS component to load, if different versions exist. A version is considered incompatible when `major version.minor version` is different from the requested version. Maybe compatible means that `build number` is different from the requested version. Finally, if `revision` is different, it is considered a QFE (Quick Fix Engineering), and generally considered compatible.

A second version number is stored in your component: the informational version. As the name implies, the informational version is considered only for documentation purposes, and its contents are something like `SuperControl Build 1890`. The informational version provides a textual representation that means something to a human, but not to the machine.

Before going on to explain private and shared NGWS components, I still owe you the command switch that you use for the compiler to add version information to your component. It is the `/a.version` switch.

```
csc /a.version:1.0.1.0 /t:library /out:wrq.dll wrq.cs
```

This creates a library with version information of 1.0.1.0. You can verify this by right-clicking the library in Explorer and inspecting the Version tab of the Properties dialog box.

Private NGWS Components

When you link an application to an NGWS component (with
`/reference:libname`), the development tool records the dependency
information, including the version of the linked libraries. This
dependency information is recorded in the manifest, and NGWS runtime
uses the contained version numbers to load the appropriate version of a
dependent NGWS component at runtime.

Do you think the NGWS components you built so far in this book were
version-checked before they were loaded? No, they weren't because any
NGWS component that resides in the application's paths is considered
private and is not version-checked. The reason for this behavior is that
you are in charge of what you place in your application directory, and
you will have tested compatibility before shipping the application.

Now, is it bad to have private NGWS components? Actually, no. There is
no way any other application could break yours by installing a shared
component because you don't use one. The only disadvantage is that your
application uses more disk space. But avoiding versioning problems in
this way is definitely worth a few bytes.

Shared NGWS Components

If you are building software you want to share between multiple
applications, you have to install it as a shared NGWS component. There
are some extra things you must take care of, however.

For starters, you need a strong name for your NGWS component. Some
of you might already have wondered where the replacement is for the
ubiquitous globally unique ID (GUID) of COM. As long as you use
private NGWS components, this is not necessary. When you start using
shared NGWS components, however, you must guarantee that their
names are unique.

Their uniqueness is guaranteed via standard public key cryptography: You
use a private key to sign your NGWS component, and applications that
link to your component have the public key to verify the component's
originator (you). After signing your NGWS component, you can deploy it
to the global NGWS component cache or the application directory. The
runtime takes care of mapping to all applications.

Is it a good idea to create a shared NGWS component? Personally, I don't think so. You once again take the risk of creating something similar to DLL Hell, although application developers depending on your component could avoid those problems by specifying binding policies. Because disk space isn't expensive today, I highly recommend using private NGWS components, and assigning strong names to them.

Summary

In this chapter, I introduced three techniques you should consider before deploying your components or applications. The first consideration is using conditional compilation. Using either the C# preprocessor or the `conditional` attribute, you can exclude or include code based on a single or several defined symbols. This enables you to conditionally compile debug versions, release versions, or whatever versions you want to build.

The documentation of your components should play an important part during development, and not just be a mere afterthought. Because C# offers you automated generation of documentation via documentation comments, I explained this feature at great length. This feature is especially useful because it enables your software to integrate its help and documentation easily with tools such as Visual Studio 7.

Finally, I talked about versioning in the NGWS runtime and its smallest unit: the NGWS component. You have a choice of creating private or shared NGWS components, but I recommend that you stick to private ones because you avoid all the problems that are associated with shared components.

CHAPTER 10

Interoperating with Unmanaged Code

- COM Interoperability
- Platform Invocation Services
- Unsafe Code

NGWS runtime is definitely a cool technology. But a cool technology isn't worth a dime if it doesn't allow you to use the (unmanaged) code that already exists, whether the code is in the form of COM components or functions implemented in C DLLs. Furthermore, sometimes managed code might get into the way of writing high-performance code—you must be able to write unmanaged, unsafe code.

NGWS and C# offer you the following techniques to interoperate with unmanaged code:

- COM Interoperability
- Platform Invocation Services
- Unsafe code

COM Interoperability

The first and most interesting interoperability technique is interoperability with COM. The reason is that for a long time to come, COM and NGWS must coexist. Your NGWS runtime clients must be able to call your legacy COM components, and COM clients must make use of new NGWS runtime components.

The following two sections deal with both issues:

- Exposing NGWS runtime objects to COM
- Exposing COM objects to the NGWS runtime

Though the interoperability discussion is centered around C#, please note that you could replace C# with VB or managed C++. It is an interoperability feature provided by the NGWS runtime to all programming languages emitting managed code.

Exposing NGWS Runtime Objects to COM

One way to interoperate is to allow a COM client to use an NGWS runtime component component (written in C#, for example). To prove the feasibility, the examples presented use the namespaced version of the `RequestWebPage` and `WhoisLookup` classes' NGWS component created in Chapter 8, "Writing Components in C#."

The various tasks involved in making an NGWS component work with a COM client are presented in the following two sections:

- Registering an NGWS Runtime object
- Invoking an NGWS Runtime object

Registering an NGWS Runtime Object

In COM, you first have to register an object before it can be used. When registering a COM object, you use the `regsvr32` application, which you obviously can't use for a COM+ 2.0 application. However, there is a similar tool for NGWS runtime components: `regasm.exe`.

The regasm tool enables you to register an NGWS component in the Registry (including all classes that are contained, given that they are publicly accessible), and it also creates a Registry file for you when you request it. The latter is useful when you want to examine what entries are added to the Registry.

The command is as follows:

```
regasm csharp.dll /reg:csharp.reg
```

The output file (csharp.reg) that is generated is shown in Listing 10.1. When you are used to COM programming, you'll recognize the entries that are being made to the Registry. Note that the ProgId is composed of the namespace and class names.

Listing 10.1   The Registry File Generated by regasm.exe

```
 1: REGEDIT4
 2:
 3: [HKEY_CLASS_ROOT\Presenting.CSharp.RequestWebPage]
 4: @="COM+ class: Presenting.CSharp.RequestWebPage"
 5:
 6: [HKEY_CLASS_ROOT\Presenting.CSharp.RequestWebPage\CLSID]
 7: @="{6B74AC4D-4489-3714-BB2E-58F9F5ADEEA3}"
 8:
 9: [HKEY_CLASS_ROOT\CLSID\{6B74AC4D-4489-3714-BB2E-58F9F5ADEEA3}]
10: @="COM+ class: Presenting.CSharp.RequestWebPage"
11:
12: [HKEY_CLASS_ROOT\CLSID\{6B74AC4D-4489-3714-BB2E-58F9F5ADEEA3}\
      ➥InprocServer32]
13: @="D:\WINNT\System32\MSCorEE.dll"
14: "ThreadingModel"="Both"
15: "Class"="Presenting.CSharp.RequestWebPage"
16: "Assembly"="csharp, Ver=1.0.1.0"
17:
18: [HKEY_CLASS_ROOT\CLSID\{6B74AC4D-4489-3714-BB2E-
➥58F9F5ADEEA3}\ProgId]
19: @="Presenting.CSharp.RequestWebPage"
20:
21: [HKEY_CLASS_ROOT\Presenting.CSharp.WhoisLookup]
22: @="COM+ class: Presenting.CSharp.WhoisLookup"
23:
24: [HKEY_CLASS_ROOT\Presenting.CSharp.WhoisLookup\CLSID]
```

continues

Listing 10.1   continued

```
25: @="{8B5D2461-07DB-3B5C-A8F9-8539A4B9BE34}"
26:
27: [HKEY_CLASS_ROOT\CLSID\{8B5D2461-07DB-3B5C-A8F9-8539A4B9BE34}]
28: @="COM+ class: Presenting.CSharp.WhoisLookup"
29:
30: [HKEY_CLASS_ROOT\CLSID\{8B5D2461-07DB-3B5C-A8F9-8539A4B9BE34}\
    ➥InprocServer32]
31: @="D:\WINNT\System32\MSCorEE.dll"
32: "ThreadingModel"="Both"
33: "Class"="Presenting.CSharp.WhoisLookup"
34: "Assembly"="csharp, Ver=1.0.1.0"
35:
36: [HKEY_CLASS_ROOT\CLSID\{8B5D2461-07DB-3B5C-A8F9-
    ➥8539A4B9BE34}\ProgId]
37: @="Presenting.CSharp.WhoisLookup"
```

Take a closer look at lines 30–34. As you can see, the execution engine
(MSCorEE.dll) is called when an instance of your object is requested, not
your library itself. The execution engine is responsible for providing the
CCW (COM Callable Wrapper) for your object.

If you want to register the component without a Registry file, all you
have to do is issue this command:

```
regasm csharp.dll
```

Now the component can be used in programming languages that support
late binding. If you are not content with late binding (and you shouldn't
be), the tlbexp utility enables you to generate a type library for your
NGWS component:

```
tlbexp csharp.dll /out:csharp.tlb
```

This type library can be used in programming languages that support
early binding. Now your NGWS component is a good citizen in COM
society.

Now that we are in the COM world, I want to dive right into the type
library and point out a few important things. I have used the OLE View
application, which comes with Visual Studio, to open the type library and
extract the IDL (Interface Description Language) of the classes contained
in the NGWS component. Listing 10.2 shows the results I obtained.

Listing 10.2   The IDL File for the WhoisLookup *and* RequestWebPage
Classes

```
 1: // Generated .IDL file (by the OLE/COM Object Viewer)
 2: //
 3: // typelib filename: <could not determine filename>
 4:
 5: [
 6:    uuid(A4466FD5-EB56-3C07-A0D8-43153AC4FD06),
 7:    version(1.0)
 8: ]
 9: library csharp
10: {
11:     // TLib :      // TLib :  : {BED7F4EA-1A96-11D2-8F08-
➡00A0C9A6186D}
12:     importlib("mscorlib.tlb");
13:     // TLib : OLE Automation : {00020430-0000-0000-C000-
➡000000000046}
14:     importlib("stdole2.tlb");
15:
16:     // Forward declare all types defined in this typelib
17:     interface _RequestWebPage;
18:     interface _WhoisLookup;
19:
20:     [
21:       uuid(6B74AC4D-4489-3714-BB2E-58F9F5ADEEA3),
22:         custom({0F21F359-AB84-41E8-9A78-36D110E6D2F9},
➡"Presenting.CSharp.RequestWebPage")
23:     ]
24:     coclass RequestWebPage {
25:         [default] interface _RequestWebPage;
26:         interface _Object;
27:     };
28:
29:     [
30:       odl,
31:       uuid(1E8F7AAB-FA6C-315B-9DFE-59C80C6483A9),
32:       hidden,
33:       dual,
34:       nonextensible,
35:       oleautomation,
36:         custom({0F21F359-AB84-41E8-9A78-36D110E6D2F9},
➡"Presenting.CSharp.RequestWebPage")
37:
```

continues

Listing 10.2   continued

```
38:     ]
39:     interface _RequestWebPage : IDispatch {
40:         [id(00000000), propget]
41:         HRESULT ToString([out, retval] BSTR* pRetVal);
42:         [id(0x60020001)]
43:         HRESULT Equals(
44:                         [in] VARIANT obj,
45:                         [out, retval] VARIANT_BOOL* pRetVal);
46:         [id(0x60020002)]
47:         HRESULT GetHashCode([out, retval] long* pRetVal);
48:         [id(0x60020003)]
49:         HRESULT GetType([out, retval] _Type** pRetVal);
50:         [id(0x60020004), propget]
51:         HRESULT URL([out, retval] BSTR* pRetVal);
52:         [id(0x60020004), propput]
53:         HRESULT URL([in] BSTR pRetVal);
54:         [id(0x60020006)]
55:         HRESULT GetContent([out] BSTR* strContent);
56:     };
57:
58:     [
59:       uuid(8B5D2461-07DB-3B5C-A8F9-8539A4B9BE34),
60:         custom({0F21F359-AB84-41E8-9A78-36D110E6D2F9},
➥"Presenting.CSharp.WhoisLookup")
61:     ]
62:     coclass WhoisLookup {
63:         [default] interface _WhoisLookup;
64:         interface _Object;
65:     };
66:
67:     [
68:       odl,
69:       uuid(07255177-A6E5-3E9F-BAB3-1B3E9833A39E),
70:       hidden,
71:       dual,
72:       nonextensible,
73:       oleautomation,
74:         custom({0F21F359-AB84-41E8-9A78-36D110E6D2F9},
➥"Presenting.CSharp.WhoisLookup")
75:
76:     ]
77:     interface _WhoisLookup : IDispatch {
78:         [id(00000000), propget]
79:         HRESULT ToString([out, retval] BSTR* pRetVal);
80:         [id(0x60020001)]
```

```
81:        HRESULT Equals(
82:                        [in] VARIANT obj,
83:                        [out, retval] VARIANT_BOOL* pRetVal);
84:        [id(0x60020002)]
85:        HRESULT GetHashCode([out, retval] long* pRetVal);
86:        [id(0x60020003)]
87:        HRESULT GetType([out, retval] _Type** pRetVal);
88:    };
89: };
```

If you are a C++ programmer, you are used to writing and maintaining such monsters. As a VB programmer, looking at such an IDL file might be a first for you.

Note that both co-classes have one IDispatch-derived interface, as well as an interface named Object (lines 24 and 62). The IDispatch default interface contains the methods you implemented in your object, plus those from the Object interface. You will also notice that now everything is using the BSTR and VARIANTs that we all know and love.

Now let's look at the interfaces in more detail. First, I want to pick the RequestWebPage interface. Figure 10.1 shows it expanded in the OLE View application.

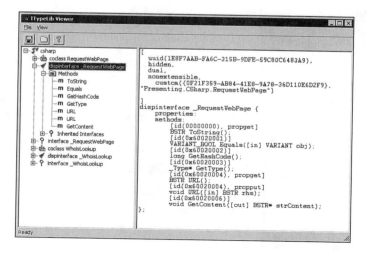

Figure 10.1

The RequestWebPage method exposes its URL property, as well as the GetContent method.

The URL property is exposed (via get and set methods), as well as the GetContent method. There are also four methods that belong to the Object interface. It looks just like it would in C# directly.

The WhoisLookup interface is a little bit different. It shows the four Object methods, but where is the Query method? (See Figure 10.2.)

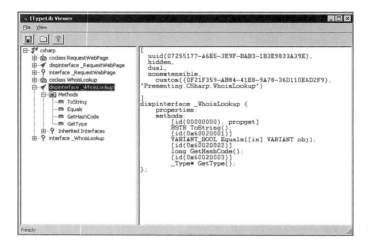

Figure 10.2

Static methods do not show up. This object cannot be used in COM.

The reason the Query method is not shown is that static methods do not show up in COM. You cannot use this object in COM unless you rewrite Query to an instance method. Therefore, if you plan to use objects outside the NGWS runtime, decide wisely which methods are static and which are instance methods.

Invoking an NGWS Runtime Object

The NGWS component and all classes are is registered, and you have a type library for environments that prefer early binding—you are all set. To demonstrate that the component works as expected, I choose Excel as the environment to script it.

To be able to use early binding in Excel, you must reference the type library. In the VBA Editor, run the References command in the Tools menu. Choose Browse in the References dialog box and then select the type library in the Add Reference dialog box (see Figure 10.3).

Figure 10.3

Importing the type library for the component.

The only task left is coding the retrieve operation. As you can see from Listing 10.3, it isn't complicated. Note that I added an On Error GoTo statement to perform the necessary COM error handling.

Listing 10.3   Using the RequestWebPage *Class in an Excel Module*

```
 1: Option Explicit
 2:
 3: Sub GetSomeInfo()
 4: On Error GoTo Err_GetSomeInfo
 5:     Dim wrq As New csharp.RequestWebPage
 6:     Dim strResult As String
 7:
 8:     wrq.URL = "http://www.alphasierrapapa.com/iisdev/"
 9:     wrq.GetContent strResult
10:     Debug.Print strResult
11:
12:     Exit Sub
13: Err_GetSomeInfo:
14:     MsgBox Err.Description
15:     Exit Sub
16: End Sub
```

NGWS runtime exceptions are translated to HRESULTs, and the exception information is passed via the error information interfaces. Excel then raises an error based on this information.

When you run the code in Listing 10.3, the output is written to the immediate window. Try entering an invalid URL to see how the exceptions are propagated from the NGWS runtime to a COM client.

Exposing COM Objects to the NGWS Runtime

Interoperation also works the other way around—NGWS runtime clients can interoperate with classic COM objects. Accessing legacy objects is the more likely scenario during the transition period from COM to NGWS.

There are two ways to access COM objects from an NGWS runtime client application:

- Invoking early-bound objects

- Invoking late-bound objects

For the examples presented in this section I chose the AspTouch component, which can change the file date of a given file. AspTouch has a dual interface and a type library, and it is free. If you want to follow the examples in this section, you can download AspTouch from `http://www.alphasierrapapa.com/iisdev/components/`.

Invoking Early-Bound Objects

For a component to be used early-bound in COM, it must have a type library. For the NGWS runtime, this translates to the metadata that is stored with the types. But wait—metadata is associated with a type, but what is the NGWS runtime type for the COM component?

To be able to call the COM component from an NGWS runtime application, you need a wrapper around the unsafe code. Such a wrapper is called an RCW (Runtime Callable Wrapper), and it is built from the type library information. A tool generates the wrapper code for you, based on the information obtained from the type library.

The tool to use is `tlbimp` (type library import). Its command line is simple:

```
tlbimp asptouch.dll /out:asptouchlib.dll
```

This command imports the COM type library from `asptouch.dll` (it is contained in the DLL as a resource), and creates and stores an RCW that can be used in the NGWS runtime in the file `asptouchlib.dll`. You can use `ildasm.exe` to view the metadata for the RCW (see Figure 10.4). Chapter 11, "Debugging C# Code," covers the use of `ILDasm` at greater length.

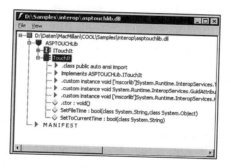

Figure 10.4

Using `ILDasm` to view the metadata of `asptouchlib.dll`.

When you look at the `ILDasm` output, you can see that `ASPTOUCHlib` is the namespace (it was the name of the type library), and `TouchIt` is the class name of the proxy that was generated for the original COM object. With this information, you can write an NGWS runtime application that uses the COM component (see Listing 10.4).

Listing 10.4   Using a COM Component in C# via an RCW

```
1: using System;
2: using ASPTOUCHLib;
3:
4: class TouchFile
5: {
6:   public static void Main()
7:   {
```

continues

Listing 10.4   continued

```
 8:    TouchIt ti = new TouchIt();
 9:    bool bResult = false;
10:    try
11:    {
12:     bResult = ti.SetToCurrentTime("asptouch.cs");
13:    }
14:    catch(Exception e)
15:    {
16:     Console.WriteLine(e);
17:    }
18:    finally
19:    {
20:     if (true == bResult)
21:     {
22:      Console.WriteLine("Successfully changed file time!");
23:     }
24:    }
25:   }
26: }
```

This code looks and feels just like any other C# code that uses a class. There is a using statement, method invocation, and exception handling (this time, the HRESULTs are wrapped as exceptions). Even the compilation command is familiar to you:

```
csc /r:asptouchlib.dll /out:touch.exe asptouch.cs
```

It works just like with any other NGWS component. After you have created the RCW, working with COM components is a walk in the park.

Invoking Late-Bound Objects

If you have a component without a type library, or you have to call it on-the-fly without prior generation of an RCW, you aren't lost at all. A cool feature of NGWS runtime will help you out: reflection. Now you can find out all about a component at runtime.

Reflection is the way to go when dealing with late-bound objects. The code in Listing 10.5 uses reflection to create the object and to invoke its methods. It performs the same actions as the previous script, but it doesn't have a wrapper class.

Listing 10.5   *Accessing a COM Component Using Reflection*

```
 1: using System;
 2: using System.Reflection;
 3:
 4: class TestLateBound
 5: {
 6:  public static void Main()
 7:  {
 8:    Type tTouch;
 9:    tTouch = Type.GetTypeFromProgID("AspTouch.TouchIt");
10:
11:    Object objTouch;
12:    objTouch = Activator.CreateInstance(tTouch);
13:
14:    Object[] parameters = new Object[1];
15:    parameters[0] = "noway.txt";
16:    bool bResult = false;
17:
18:    try
19:    {
20:     bResult = (bool)tTouch.InvokeMember("SetToCurrentTime",
21:      BindingFlags.InvokeMethod,
22:      null, objTouch, parameters);
23:    }
24:    catch(Exception e)
25:    {
26:     Console.WriteLine(e);
27:    }
28:
29:    if (bResult)
30:     Console.WriteLine("Changed successfully!");
31:  }
32: }
```

The class to use for reflection is Type, which is included in the
System.Reflection namespace. Line 9 then calls GetTypeFromProgID
with the ProgId of the COM component in question to get the
component's type. Although I don't check for an exception, you should
do so; an exception is thrown if the type could not be loaded.

Now that the type is loaded, I can create an instance of it by using the
CreateInstance static method of the Activator class. The TouchIt
object is ready to be used. But the really ugly part of late-bound
programming has just begun—invoking methods.

If you loved late-bound programming with C++ and COM, you'll find yourself at home with this code immediately. All parameters—in this case, the name of the file—must be packaged in an array (lines 14–15), and the call to the method is performed indirectly via the `InvokeMember` of the `Type` object (lines 20–22). You have to pass it the name of the method, the binding flags, a binder, the object, and finally, the parameters. The result returned by the invocation must be cast to the appropriate type of C#/NGWS runtime.

Looks and feels ugly, doesn't it? And the call I use in this example is not even the most complicated one you can come up with. Passing parameters by reference is much more fun, I promise.

Although the complexity of working with late-bound objects is manageable after all, there is exactly one reason why you always should work with RCWs instead: speed. Late-bound invocation is a magnitude slower than working with early-bound objects.

Platform Invocation Services

Even with all the NGWS framework classes and COM Interoperability, you sometimes might feel the need to call a single function provided by WIN32 or some other unmanaged DLL. This is the time when you might want to use the Platform Invocation Services (`PInvoke`). `PInvoke` takes care of finding and invoking the correct function, as well as marshaling its managed arguments to and from their unmanaged counterparts.

All you have to do to is use the `sysimport` attribute when defining an `extern` method in C#:

```
[sysimport(
   dll=dllname,
   name=entrypoint,
   charset=character set
)]
```

Only the `dll` argument is mandatory; both other arguments are optional. If you omit the `name` attribute, the name of the externally implemented function must match the name of the internal static method.

Listing 10.6 demonstrates how to invoke the message box function of WIN32 using `PInvoke`.

Listing 10.6 *Using `PInvoke` to Call WIN32 Functions*

```
1: using System;
2:
3: class TestPInvoke
4: {
5:  [sysimport(dll="user32.dll")]
6:  public static extern int MessageBoxA(int hWnd, string strMsg,
7:      string strCaption, int nType);
8:
9:  public static void Main()
10: {
11:   int nMsgBoxResult;
12:   nMsgBoxResult = MessageBoxA(0, "Hello C#", "PInvoke", 0);
13: }
14: }
```

Line 5 uses the `sysimport` attribute to specify that the function I am going to call is declared in `user32.dll`. Because I do not specify a `name` argument, the following definition for the `extern` method must exactly match the name of the function I want to call: `MessageBoxA`, where `A` is for the ANSI version of this function. The output of this simple application is a message box with a `"Hello C#"` message.

Listing 10.7 demonstrates that by using the `name` argument, you can rename the `extern` method to your liking.

Listing 10.7 *Modifying the `sysimport` Attribute Still Yields the Desired Result*

```
1: using System;
2:
3: class TestPInvoke
4: {
5:  [sysimport(dll="user32.dll", name="MessageBoxA")]
6:  public static extern int PopupBox(int h, string m, string c,
➡int type);
7:
8:  public static void Main()
9:  {
10:   int nMsgBoxResult;
```

continues

Listing 10.7   continued

```
11:    nMsgBoxResult = PopupBox(0, "Hello C#", "PInvoke", 0);
12:  }
13: }
```

Although I demonstrated only a very straightforward and simple WIN32 method, you can invoke any method that comes to your mind. If you get extremely fancy, you can access WIN32 resource data or implement your own data marshaling. For this, however, you have to take a look into the SDK documentation of NGWS runtime.

Unsafe Code

Programming unsafe code yourself is definitely not a task you will perform every day when using C#. However, it is good to know that you can use pointers when you have to do so. C# supports you with two keywords for writing unsafe code:

- unsafe—This keyword denotes an unsafe context. When you want to perform unsafe actions, you must wrap the corresponding code with this modifier. It can be applied to constructors, methods, and properties.

- fixed—Declaring a variable as fixed prevents the garbage collector from relocating it.

Unless you really need to work with raw blocks of memory—with pointers, that is—COM Interoperability and the Platform Invocation Services should cover almost all your needs to talk to COM or WIN32 functions.

To give you an idea what unsafe code might look like, take a look at Listing 10.8. It shows how to use the unsafe and fixed keywords to create a program that performs the square calculation just a little bit differently. To learn more about writing unsafe code, please take a look at the C# reference.

Listing 10.8   Working with Unsafe Code

```
 1: using System;
 2:
 3: public class SquareSampleUnsafe
 4: {
 5:   unsafe public void CalcSquare(int nSideLength, int *pResult)
 6:   {
 7:     *pResult = nSideLength * nSideLength;
 8:   }
 9: }
10:
11: class TestUnsafe
12: {
13:   public static void Main()
14:   {
15:     int nResult = 0;
16:
17:     unsafe
18:     {
19:      fixed(int* pResult = &nResult)
20:      {
21:       SquareSampleUnsafe sqsu = new SquareSampleUnsafe();
22:       sqsu.CalcSquare(15,pResult);
23:       Console.WriteLine(nResult);
24:      }
25:     }
26:   }
27: }
```

Summary

This chapter was entirely about how managed code can interoperate with unmanaged code. At first, you learned how COM Interoperability can make NGWS components work with COM clients, as well as how you can use COM components in NGWS runtime clients. You learned about the differences of calling an object with late binding or early binding, and what metadata and type libraries look like for the conversion process.

A further interoperability service is the Platform Invocation Service PInvoke. It enables you to call WIN32 functions, and it takes care of the data marshaling for you. However, if you want to do it on your own, PInvoke allows you to do so.

The last feature presented is unsafe code. Although C# prefers managed code, you still can work with pointers, pin blocks of memory to a specific location, and do all the stuff you always wanted to do but that managed C# didn't allow.

CHAPTER 11

Debugging C# Code

- Debugging Tasks
- The Intermediate Language Disassembler

How many times do you write code, run it once to verify the result, and then declare the code tested? I hope that doesn't happen too often. You should test your code line-by-line using a debugger. Even then, you can prove only the existence of bugs, but not their absence.

Debugging is an important task in the software development process. The NGWS SDK provides tools that enable you to debug your components thoroughly. My recommendation: Use them! This chapter tells you how to use the following two tools:

- The SDK debugger
- The IL Disassembler

Debugging Tasks

Two debuggers ship with the NGWS SDK: a command-line debugger named CORDBG and a UI debugger named SDK debugger. The latter is a stripped-down version of the Visual Studio 7 debugger, and it is the one discussed in this chapter. The SDK debugger has the following limitations when compared to its Visual Studio counterpart:

- The SDK debugger doesn't support debugging of native code. You can debug only managed code.

- No remote machine debugging is supported. To debug code on a remote machine, you must use the Visual Studio debugger.

- The Registers window, although implemented, is not functional.

- The Disassembly window, although implemented, is not functional.

These limitations are of concern only when you debug in mixed-language or remote environments. For the bulk of debugging tasks, the SDK debugger is just fine when

- Creating a debug version of your application

- Selecting the executable

- Setting breakpoints

- Stepping through your program

- Attaching to a process

- Inspecting and modifying variables

- Managing exception handling

- JIT debugging

- Debugging components

Creating a Debug Version of Your Application

The first step you must take before you can debug your application code is to create a debug version of your application. The debug build contains debugging information, is not optimized, and an additional PDB (program database) file for debugging and project state information is created.

To create such a debug build, you add two switches to the compilation process:

```
csc /optimize- /debug+ whilesample.cs
```

This command creates two files: `whilesample.exe` and `whilesample.pdb`. Now your application is ready to be debugged. Listing 11.1 contains the source code of `whilesample.cs` for your review, as it is used again in the upcoming sections.

Listing 11.1   The `whilesample.cs` *File Used for Debugging*

```
 1: using System;
 2: using System.IO;
 3:
 4: class WhileDemoApp
 5: {
 6:   public static void Main()
 7:   {
 8:     StreamReader sr = File.OpenText ("whilesample.cs");
 9:     String strLine = null;
10:
11:     while (null != (strLine = sr.ReadLine()))
12:     {
13:         Console.WriteLine(strLine);
14:     }
15:
16:     sr.Close();
17:   }
18: }
```

Selecting the Executable

The first step in setting up a debugging session is to select which application you want to debug. Although you can attach to already-running applications (shown later), the usual case is that you know upfront which application to debug. Therefore, you start that application from inside the debugger.

You have already built one application for debugging in the previous section: whilesample.exe. You now set up the SDK debugger (shown in Figure 11.1) to debug it. To start the SDK debugger, execute the application DbgUrt.exe, which resides in the folder *drive*:\Program Files\NGWSSDK\GuiDebug.

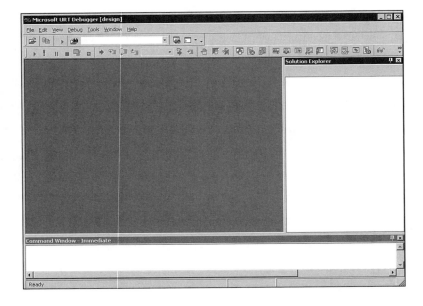

Figure 11.1

The SDK debugger main window.

To select an executable for the debugging session, open the Debug menu and choose the Program to Debug menu item. In the Program To Debug dialog box, select the appropriate program by using the browse button (its caption is ...) next to the Program text box (see Figure 11.2).

Figure 11.2

Selecting the executable for the debugging session.

Note that you can also specify command-line arguments in the Arguments text box, which are passed to the application when the debugging session is started. Because the current application does not take any arguments, leave this text box empty.

Basically, you could start the application in debugging mode immediately. However, it is a good idea to define where you want to start inspecting the code during execution by setting breakpoints.

Setting Breakpoints

You can set four types of breakpoints in your applications:

- File breakpoint—Breaks execution when a specified location (line number) in a source file is reached.

- Data breakpoint—Breaks execution when a variable (for example, a counter in a loop) changes to a specified value.

- Function breakpoint—Breaks execution at a specific location within a specified function.

- Address breakpoint—Breaks execution when a specified memory address is reached during execution.

The most commonly used kind of breakpoint is definitely the file breakpoint. Complete the following two steps to create a file breakpoint for line 11 of whilesample.cs, which is the start of the while loop.

1. From the File menu, choose Open/File. Search for the file
   `whilesample.cs` and open it.

2. Go to the line where you want to place the breakpoint and right-
   click. Select Insert Breakpoint from the context menu. Your SDK
   debugger window should now resemble the one in Figure 11.3. A
   red dot next to the line indicates that the line contains a breakpoint
   (except in the case of data breakpoints).

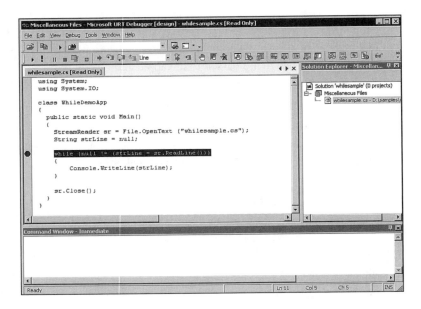

Figure 11.3

Defining a breakpoint in the SDK debugger.

That is all there is to adding a breakpoint. If you want to edit the
breakpoint's properties, simply right-click and then select Breakpoint
Properties from the context menu. There you can set a breakpoint
condition and click Count. This technique can be used to tell the
debugger to break at the breakpoint when the breakpoint condition is
satisfied for the *n*th time.

If you want to gain a quick overview of which breakpoints are set and
which conditions and hit counts are defined, simply open the Breakpoints

window. It can be accessed via the Windows/Breakpoints option in the Debug menu (see Figure 11.4).

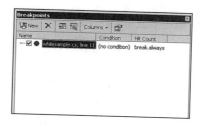

Figure 11.4

Inspecting a breakpoint in the Breakpoints window.

With a breakpoint defined, you can now start the program in debugging mode. Either select Start from the Debug menu, or click the play-button-like symbol on the Debug toolbar. Execution will break at your breakpoint, enabling you to step through your application.

Stepping Through Your Program

The execution of your application is halted at a breakpoint, and you are in charge of how the application continues to run. You can execute the code statements by using the following commands (available via the Debug toolbar or menu):

- Step Over—Executes a single statement, including a simple assignment or a function call.

- Step Into—Differs from the Step Over command in that if a function is in the executed line, the debugger steps into the function. This enables you to debug function calls.

- Step Out—Enables you to step out of a function and return to the calling function.

- Run to Cursor—Executes all statements up to the point where you place the input cursor. Breakpoints between the current break position and the cursor location are honored.

Give the various commands a try in the current debugging session. When done, close the debugger.

Attaching to a Process

Instead of specifying the executable upfront for the debugging session, you can pick one from the list of currently executing applications and attach to that application to debug it. This works for applications either that are executed as a service, or that depend on user interaction. Basically, the point is that you must have enough time to attach to the application before it finishes executing.

To demonstrate how this works, I will reuse the do-while example that prompts the user to enter numbers to compute an average (see Listing 11.2).

Listing 11.2   The attachto.cs *File for Demonstrating Process Attaching*

```
 1: using System;
 2:
 3: class ComputeAverageApp
 4: {
 5:  public static void Main()
 6:  {
 7:   ComputeAverageApp theApp = new ComputeAverageApp();
 8:   theApp.Run();
 9:  }
10:
11:  public void Run()
12:  {
13:   double dValue = 0;
14:   double dSum = 0;
15:   int nNoOfValues = 0;
16:   char chContinue = 'y';
17:   string strInput;
18:
19:   do
20:   {
21:    Console.Write("Enter a value: ");
22:    strInput = Console.ReadLine();
23:    dValue = Double.Parse(strInput);
24:    dSum += dValue;
```

```
25:    nNoOfValues++;
26:    Console.Write("Read another value?");
27:
28:    strInput = Console.ReadLine();
29:    chContinue = Char.FromString(strInput);
30:    }
31:    while ('y' == chContinue);
32:
33:    Console.WriteLine("The average is {0}",dSum / nNoOfValues);
34:    }
35: }
```

Compile it using the following command (just a reminder):

```
csc /optimize- /debug+ attachto.cs
```

Execute the application at the command prompt and wait until it shows the Enter a value: prompt. Then switch to the SDK debugger.

In the NGWS RUNTIME Debugger, choose Programs from the Debug menu. This opens the Programs dialog box, where you can choose the application that you want to debug (see Figure 11.5). Note that the SDK debugger can only be used to debug applications that are of type COM+.

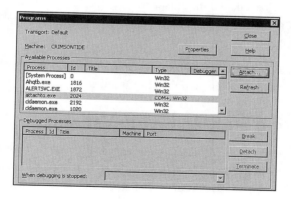

Figure 11.5

Attaching to a running program.

Click the Attach button, and click OK in the Attach to Process dialog box that opens. Note that the Programs dialog box has now changed (see

Figure 11.6). A welcome addition is that you can choose either to detach from the process when you are finished debugging, or to simply terminate it.

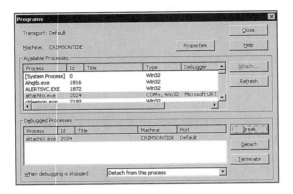

Figure 11.6

You can choose how to detach from a process after you have attached to it.

For now, click the Break button and then click Close. The source file is automatically loaded, and the cursor waits in the line where the application is waiting for the user input. Switch back to the application window, and enter a numeric value.

The next section continues with this sample. It shows you how to read and change values that are assigned to variables.

Inspecting and Modifying Variables

When you return to the SDK debugger, you will notice that the debugger is still waiting in the `Console.ReadLine` line. Step over it to read in the value you entered. Place the cursor in line 26 and select Run to Cursor. All calculation code is executed.

Because this section is about inspecting and modifying variables, let's begin to do so. Open the Locals window via the Debug, Windows/Locals menu option. The Locals window shows all variables that are local to the currently executing method (see Figure 11.7).

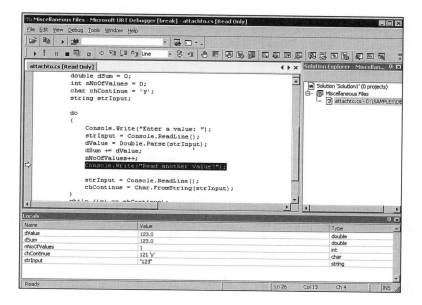

Figure 11.7

Viewing the variables that are local to the current method.

To modify a variable's value, double-click in the Value column of that variable. Enter a new value and press the Enter key. That's all you have to do.

Another window of interest is Watch. In contrast to the Locals window, Watch doesn't show any variables by default. You must enter the variables you want to watch by clicking the Name column and entering the variable's name. However, the variables always stay in the Watch window even if you jump between methods. Use the Watch window to track variables of interest.

Managing Exception Handling

A really cool feature of the SDK debugger is how you can deal with exceptions. With an application selected for debugging, you can open the configuration window for exceptions via the Debug, Exceptions menu choice. Figure 11.8 shows the Exceptions dialog where you can configure how the debugger should react to various exceptions.

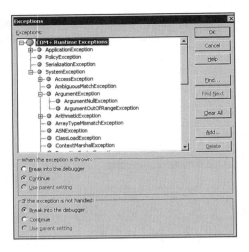

Figure 11.8

Defining how the SDK debugger should react to different exceptions.

The default setting is to continue execution when an exception is thrown and, if the exception is not handled by your code, to break into the debugger. All listed exceptions inherit this default—their Use Parent Setting radio button is selected.

Although the defaults in place enable you to find exceptions that are not handled in your code, you might feel the need to change the behavior for certain exceptions. You might want to continue execution when an argument exception is thrown but not handled, or you might decide to break into the debugger automatically when a `FileIOException` is thrown (before the handler is invoked).

JIT Debugging

Exceptions are an excellent starting point for a debugging session anyway. When an exception is not handled properly by your code, you are prompted to start debugging (see Figure 11.9). This is called JIT (just in time) debugging.

Figure 11.9

Exceptions enable you to JIT debug your application.

The SDK debugger starts when you choose to perform JIT debugging. Give your okay to attach to the process in question, and the debugger automatically opens the source file and places the cursor in the offending line. In addition, you are notified about which exception has occurred (see Figure 11.10).

You can now debug the application to your heart's content by using the techniques that were outlined in this chapter.

Debugging Components

Debugging C# components isn't that different from debugging components written in C++: You must attach to a client application that uses the component, and then add breakpoints to the component's source code (or wait for an exception). The client application need not be compiled for use in debugging mode, but I recommend this.

Once again, the namespaced version of our component DLL is used as an example. The compiler switches are as follows:

```
csc /r:System.Net.dll /t:library /out:csharp.dll /a.version:1.0.1.0
➡/debug+ /optimize- whoisns.cs wrqns.cs
```

Write a client application, and compile it as a debug version:

```
csc /r:csharp.dll /out:wrq.exe /debug+ /optimize- wrqclientns.cs
```

You are now free either to start the client application in a debugging session, or to start it in a command window and then attach to it. When both the client and the component are written in managed code and are compiled as a debug version, you can step from client code into component code.

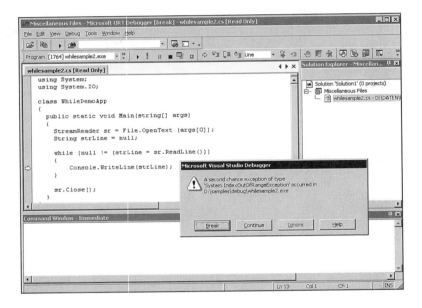

Figure 11.10

The debugger tells you which exception caused the JIT debugging session.

The Intermediate Language Disassembler

A nifty tool that comes with the NGWS SDK is the Intermediate Language (IL) Disassembler, or ILDasm. Despite the task that its name implies, you can use the IL Disassembler to gain important knowledge about the metadata and manifests of your NGWS executables. Use this tool, for example, when you have created an RCW (Runtime Callable Wrapper) for a COM component and want to learn more about the wrapper class.

You can start the IL Disassembler from the Tools submenu of the Microsoft NGWS SDK start menu. Initially, the window is empty, but when you select an NGWS component via the File, Open menu option, all types are displayed and you can browse the namespaces (see Figure 11.11).

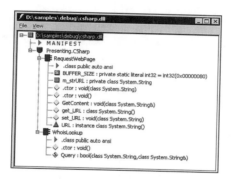

Figure 11.11

Using ILDasm to browse an NGWS component.

When you double-click MANIFEST, you can see which libraries were imported, and gain information (version number, and so on) about the manifest for the component itself.

A feature for advanced programmers who really want to know more is that ILDasm can show the IL assembly code that was generated for a specific method (see Figure 11.12). Because it is annotated with the actual C# source code (debug only), you can easily learn how IL works. The IL instructions are documented in the NGWS SDK.

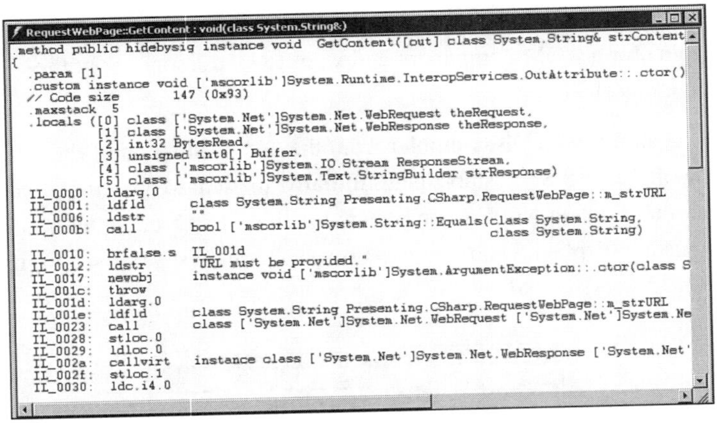

Figure 11.12

Viewing the IL for the GetContent *method.*

Summary

In this chapter, you learned how to use the SDK debugger that ships with the NGWS SDK. Because the SDK debugger is a minimally stripped-down version of the Visual Studio debugger, it provides a wealth of debugging functionality, which makes it a snap to test your applications.

You can start a debugging session with a certain executable, or you can attach to one that is already running. On hitting a breakpoint, you can step into, step out of, step over, or run to a cursor position. Variable inspection and modification are, of course, also possible. With the very flexible exception handling provided, you can very thoroughly examine your application.

For those who like assembly language, the IL Disassembler is a tool they'll really enjoy—they can easily learn the IL statements and interpret the code. For the rest of us, the IL Disassembler is an important tool to learn more about a component's manifest and metadata.

CHAPTER 12

Security

- Code Access Security
- Role-Based Security

Security is an important topic, especially so because today's code comes from multiple sources, including the Internet. Therefore, addressing security needs was an important design goal for NGWS. These needs are addressed on the code level itself, as well as on the user permission level.

Because the security provided by NGWS could fill a book on its own, this chapter only introduces you to the concepts and possibilities. There are no code examples. I don't want to convey the false impression that security is an afterthought, and short, unrelated examples would give that impression.

Therefore, the following topics are covered in this chapter from a conceptual viewpoint:

- Code-access security
- Role-based security

Code-Access Security

Today, code can come to a user's desk not only via a setup application executed from a company's network server, but also from the Internet via a Web page or an email. Recent experiences have shown that this can be quite dangerous. So how can this threat be answered with NGWS?

The NGWS solution is code-access security. It controls access to protected resources and operations. Code is trusted to varying degrees, depending on its identity and where it comes from. The amount of code that must be fully trusted is reduced to a minimum.

The following are the most notable functions of code access security:

- Administrators can define security policies that assign certain permissions to defined groups of code.

- Code can demand that a caller must have specific permissions.

- Code execution is restricted by the runtime. Checks are performed that verify the granted permissions of a caller match the required permissions for the operations.

- Code can request the permissions it requires to run and the permissions that would be useful, as well as explicitly state which permissions it must never have.

- Permissions are defined that represent certain rights to access various system resources.

- Code-access security grants permissions when a component is loaded. This granting is based on the requests by the code, as well as the permitted operations defined by the security policy.

From reading this list, you can see that less-trusted code will be prevented from calling highly trusted code because permissions of the less-trusted code are enforced. You will especially like that for Internet scenarios.

The two important points of code-access security are verification of the type safety of managed code, and the permissions that are requested by the code. The minimum requirement for you to benefit from code-access security is to generate type-safe code.

Verification of Type Safety

The first step for the runtime in enforcing security restrictions on managed code is being able to determine whether the code is type safe. This matters because the runtime must be able to check the permissions of callers reliably.

The runtime checks permissions for all callers in the call stack to circumvent the security hole that is created when less-trusted code calls highly trusted code. For this stack-walking, the managed code must be verifiably type safe—every access to types is performed only in allowed ways.

The good news is that the C# code you write is type safe unless you want to write unsafe code. Both the IL and the metadata are inspected before the okay is given regarding the type safety of code.

Permissions

The next step is to work actively with permissions. The benefit from actively requesting permissions is that you know when you have proper permissions to perform your code's actions, or how to degrade gracefully when you don't get them. Additionally, you can prevent your code from getting extra permissions it wouldn't need. Minimal permissions guarantee that your code will run on tightly restricted systems where code that requests too much permission without need will fail.

Although I mentioned the kinds of permissions already, here is the list again:

- Required—Permissions that your code needs to run properly.

- Optional—Permissions that are not mandatory for the proper execution of your code, but that would be good to have.

- Refused—Permissions that you want to ensure your code is never granted—even if the security policy would allow it. You can use this to restrict potential vulnerabilities.

The interesting question is which permissions can be requested by code, which permissions are granted by the code's identity, and which permissions derive from the user's identity. Only the first two belong to code-access security; the latter is tied to role-based security.

Therefore, the two kinds of code-access security permissions are

- Standard permissions

- Identity permissions

Standard Permissions

Securing access to resources that are exposed by the NGWS framework is taken care of by the code-access permissions. With those permissions, you gain either access to a protected resource, or the right to perform a protected operation. Your code can demand any permission at runtime, and the runtime decides whether your code gets that permission.

Table 12.1 shows a list of standard permissions and a brief description of each. Note, for example, that the net classes have separate network access security.

Table 12.1 *Standard Permissions*

Permission	Description
EnvironmentPermission	This class defines access permissions to environment variables. Two types of access are possible: read-only access to the value of an environment variable, and write access. Write access includes permissions to create and delete environment variables.
FileDialogPermission	Controls access to files based on the system file dialog. The user must authorize the file access via that dialog.

Permission	Description
FileIOPermission	Three different types of file I/O access may be specified: read, write, and append. Read access includes access to file information; write access includes delete and overwrite; and append access limits you to appending—you are not allowed to read other bits.
IsolatedStoragePermission	Controls access to the isolated storage (per user). Restrictions include allowed usage, storage quota size, expiration of data, and data retaining.
ReflectionPermission	Controls the capability to read the type information of nonpublic members of types. In addition, it controls the use of Reflection.Emit.
RegistryPermission	Reading, creating, and writing in the Registry are controlled with this permission. Each type of access must be specified separately for a list of keys and values.
SecurityPermission	SecurityPermission is a collection of simple permission flags that are used by the security system. You can control the execution of code, override of security checks, invocation of unmanaged code, verification skipping, serialization, and more.
UIPermission	Defines the access to various aspects of the user interface, including the use of windows, access to events, as well as the use of the Clipboard.

Identity Permissions

Identity permissions cannot be requested—they are granted based on evidence from the application code. This kind of permission is a secure way for NGWS to determine the identity of managed code, including its origin (possibly a Web site) and its publisher, based on the signature of the code.

Table 12.2 shows the identity permissions and their descriptions.

Table 12.2 *Identity Permissions*

Permission	Description
`PublisherIdentityPermission`	The signature on an NGWS component provides proof of the software's publisher.
`StrongNameIdentityPermission`	Defines the cryptographically strong name of a component. The strong name key and the simple name part comprise the identity.
`ZoneIdentityPermission`	Defines the zone from which the code originates. A URL can belong to only one zone.
`SiteIdentityPermission`	Permissions derived based on the Web site from which the code originates.
`URLIdentityPermission`	Permissions derived based on the URL from which the code originates.

Role-Based Security

The system of role-based security might be already familiar for you because the NGWS role-based security system is, to some degree, similar to the one found in COM+. However, there are some differences you need to be aware of, so read on.

The NGWS role-based security is modeled around a principal, which represents either a user, or an agent that is acting on behalf of a given user. An NGWS application makes security decisions based on either the principal's identity, or its role membership.

So, what is a role? For example, a bank has clerks and managers. A clerk can prepare a loan application, but the manager must approve it. It doesn't matter which instance of manager (principal) approves it, but he or she must be a member of the manager role.

In more technical terms, a *role* is a named set of users who share the same privileges. One principal can be a member of multiple roles and, therefore, you can use role membership to determine whether certain requested actions may be performed for a principal.

I have already mentioned briefly that a principal is not necessarily a user, but it can be also an agent. More generally, there are three kinds of principals:

- Generic principals—These represent unauthenticated users, as well as the roles available to them.

- Windows principals—Map to Windows users and their groups (roles). Impersonation (accessing a resource on another user's behalf) is supported.

- Custom principals—Defined by an application. They can extend the basic notion of the identity and the roles that the principal is in. The restriction is that your application must provide an authentication module as well as the types that implement the principal.

How does it work for you in your application? NGWS provides you with the `PrincipalPermission` class, which provides consistency with code-access security. It enables the runtime to perform authorization in a way similar to code-access security checks, but you can directly access a principal's identity information and perform role and identity checks in your code when you need to do so.

Summary

In this final chapter of this book, I introduced you to the concepts of security that are part of NGWS. I took you on a tour of code-access security and role-based security. You learned about standard and identity permissions, which are used to enforce code-access security, as well as about principals and roles in role-based security scenarios.

INDEX

Symbols

A

B

C

G - H

generic principals, role-based security, 191
GetContent method (RequestWebPage class), 112-115
goto case label in switch statements, 85-86

Hello World program
    code blocks (statements), 33
    compiling, 35-36
    Console object
        input/output methods, 36-38
        WriteLine method, 34
    Main method, 33
    namespace, importing, 35
    statements (code blocks), 33
hiding methods, 64-66

I - J

identifiers, Common Language Specification (CLS), 27
if statement
    Boolean expressions, 80-83
    comparison operators, 81
    else branches, 80
    letter case determination example, 81-83
    potential danger in certain values, 83
IL (Intermediate Language), 35-36
    CPU independence, 17
    instruction categories, 18
    native code, converting (JITters), 18-19
    portable executable (PE) format, 18
importing namespaces
    client applications, 120-123
    Hello World program, 35
in parameters (methods), 59-60
indexers (classes)
    declarator, 68-70
    IP address retrieval example, 69-70
    syntax, 68-70

IndexOutOfRangeException type, 106
input methods, Console object (Hello World program), 36-37
int return type (Main method), 34
int type (integral value type), 43
integral value types, 43
interfaces
    abstract members, 49-50
    Common Language Specification (CLS), 27
Intermediate Language, *see* IL
Intermediate Language Disassembler (ILDasm)
    component manifest, 183
    launching, 183
    metadata, 182
internal access modifiers, 76
Internet Explorer, XML documentation files, viewing, 145-147
InteropException type, 106
InvalidOperationException type, 106
invoking
    NGWS objects with COM, 158-160
    early-bound objects, 160-162
    late-bound objects, 162-164
IP addresses, class indexer example, 69-70
IsolatedStoragePermission (code-access security), 189
iteration statements, 87
    do, 92-93
    for, 87-89
    foreach, 89-90
    while, 91

JIT Compiler Manager (jitman.exe), 20-21
JIT debugging, exceptions, 180-181
JITters (Just-in-Time compilers), 18-19
    JIT Compiler Manager (jitman.exe), 20-21
    types
        EconoJIT, 19
        JIT, 19
        PreJIT, 19

L - M

N

O

P

S

X - Y - Z

W